# RON

The L. Ron Hubbard Series

Bridge Publications, Inc.
5600 E. Olympic Blvd.
Commerce, California 90022 USA

ISBN 978-1-4031-9899-0



Cover artwork & illustrations: pp. 41, 138, 139, 141 *Unknown & Astounding Science Fiction* copyright © by Street & Smith Publications, Inc. Reprinted with permission of Penny Publications, LLC; pp. 138, 139 *Argosy Magazine* is © 1936, 1937 Argosy Communications, Inc. All Rights Reserved. Reprinted with permission from Argosy Communications, Inc.; pp. 138, 139 © 1948, 1949 Standard Magazine, Inc., and Better Publications, Inc. Reprinted with permission of Hachette Filipacchi Media; pp. 138, 139 © and ™ Condé Nast Publications and are used with their permission.

Special acknowledgment is made to the L. Ron Hubbard Library for permission to reproduce photographs from his personal collection. Additional credits: pp. 23, 44 National Archives; pp. 50–51 © Earl Theisen/Roxann Livingston; pp. 65, 66 (upper left & middle), 67, 68 Keystone Press Agency/Hulton Archive; p. 66 (upper right & lower) Ken Lauder/Rex Features Ltd.; p. 72 Barratts Photo Press Ltd.; pp. 84–85 Tetra Images/Getty Images; pp. 87, 93, 97, 105, 109, 113, 121, 137, 149, 153 Dman/Shutterstock.com; p. 89 Sura Nualpradid/Shutterstock.com; p. 137 Pagina/Shutterstock.com; p. 141 (second cover) © 2012 Cliff Nielsen; pp. 142, 143 © 2007 Cliff Nielsen; p. 146 © 2010 Cliff Nielsen; p. 149 norbi/Shutterstock.com; p. 153 Topal/Shutterstock.com.

Article appearing on page 66 courtesy of *Garden News.*



*Printed in the United States of America*

The L. Ron Hubbard Series: L. Ron Hubbard: A Profile—English

The L. Ron Hubbard Series

# L. RON HUBBARD
# A PROFILE

*Bridge*

PUBLICATIONS, INC. ®

# CONTENTS

## *An Introduction to*
# L. Ron Hubbard

THERE ARE ONLY TWO TESTS OF A LIFE WELL LIVED, L. RON Hubbard once remarked: Did one do as one intended? And were people glad one lived? In testament to the first stands the full body of his life's work, including the more than ten thousand authored works and three thousand tape-recorded lectures of Dianetics and Scientology. In evidence of the second are the hundreds of millions whose lives have been demonstrably bettered because he lived. They are the generations of students now reading superlatively, owing to L. Ron Hubbard's educational discoveries; they are the millions more freed from the lure of substance abuse through L. Ron Hubbard's breakthroughs in drug rehabilitation; still more touched by his common sense moral code; and many millions more again who hold his work as the spiritual cornerstone of their lives.

Although best known for Dianetics and Scientology, L. Ron Hubbard cannot be so simply categorized. If nothing else, his life was too varied, his influence too broad. There are tribesmen in Southern Africa, for example, who know nothing of Dianetics and Scientology, but they know L. Ron Hubbard, the educator. Similarly, there are factory workers across Eastern Europe who know him only for his administrative discoveries; children in Southeast Asia who know him only as the author of their moral code and readers in dozens of languages who know him only for his novels. So, no, L. Ron Hubbard is not an easy man to categorize and certainly does not fit popular misconceptions of "religious founder" as an aloof and contemplative figure. Yet the more one comes to know this man and his achievements, the more one comes to realize he was precisely the sort of person to have brought us Scientology—the only major religion to have been founded in the twentieth century.

What Scientology offers is likewise what one would expect of a man such as L. Ron Hubbard. For not only does it provide circulation, including such monumental bestsellers as *Fear, Final Blackout, Battlefield Earth* and the ten-volume *Mission Earth* series,

> *"So how would we expect to characterize the founder of such a religion? Clearly, he would have to be larger than life, attracted to people, liked by people, dynamic, charismatic and immensely capable in a dozen fields—all exactly L. Ron Hubbard."*

an entirely unique approach to our most fundamental questions—Who are we? From where did we come and what is our destiny?—but it further provides an equally unique technology for greater spiritual freedom. So how would we expect to characterize the founder of such a religion? Clearly, he would have to be larger than life, attracted to people, liked by people, dynamic, charismatic and immensely capable in a dozen fields—all exactly L. Ron Hubbard.

The fact is, if Mr. Hubbard had stopped after only one of his many accomplishments, he would still be celebrated today. For example, with some fifty million works of fiction in

Mr. Hubbard is unquestionably among the most acclaimed and widely read authors of all time. His novels additionally earned some of the literature's most prestigious awards and he is very truthfully described as "one of the most prolific and influential writers of the twentieth century."

His earlier accomplishments are equally impressive. As a barnstorming aviator through the 1930s, he was known as "Flash Hubbard" and broke all local records for sustained glider flight. As a leader of far-flung expeditions, he is credited with conducting the first complete Puerto Rican mineralogical survey under United States protectorship and his navigational annotations still influence the maritime guides for British Columbia. His experimentation with early radio directional finding further became the basis for the LOng RAnge Navigation system (LORAN); while as a lifelong photographer, his work was featured in *National Geographic* and his exhibits drew tens of thousands.

Among other avenues of research, Mr. Hubbard developed and codified an administrative technology that is utilized by organizations of every description, including multinational corporations, charitable bodies, political parties, schools, youth clubs and every imaginable small business. Likewise Mr. Hubbard's internationally acclaimed educational methods are utilized by educators from every academic quarter, while his equally acclaimed drug rehabilitation program routinely proves doubly and even triply more effective than any similarly aimed program.

Yet however impressive these facts of his life, no measure of the man is replete without some appreciation of what became his life's

*"The Story is immense, wondrous and effectively encompasses the whole of his existence."*

work: Dianetics and Scientology. (See the L. Ron Hubbard Series edition, *Philosopher & Founder: Rediscovery of the Human Soul.*)

The story is immense, wondrous and effectively encompasses the whole of his existence. Yet the broad strokes are these: By way of a first entrance into a spiritual dimension, he tells of a boyhood friendship with indigenous Blackfeet Indians in Helena, Montana. Notable among them was a full-fledged tribal medicine man locally known as Old Tom. In what ultimately constituted a rare bond, the six-year-old Ron was both honored with the status of blood brother and instilled with an appreciation of a profoundly distinguished spiritual heritage.

What may be seen as the next milestone came in 1923 when a twelve-year-old L. Ron Hubbard began an examination of Freudian theory with a Commander Joseph C. Thompson—the only United States naval officer to study with Freud in Vienna. Although neither the young nor later Ron Hubbard was to ever accept psychoanalysis per se, the exposure once again proved pivotal. For if nothing else, as Mr. Hubbard phrased it, Freud at least advanced an idea that "something could be done about the mind."

The third crucial step of this journey lay in Asia, where an L. Ron Hubbard, then still in his teens, spent the better part of two years in travel and study. He became one of the few Americans of the age to gain entrance into fabled Tibetan lamaseries scattered through the Western Hills of China and actually studied with the last in a line of royal magicians descended from the court of Kublai Khan. Yet however enthralling were such adventures, he would finally admit to finding nothing either workable or predictable as regards the human mind. Hence his summary statement on abiding misery in lands where wisdom is great but carefully hidden and only doled out as superstition.

Upon his return to the United States in 1929 and completion of his high-school education, Mr. Hubbard enrolled in George Washington University. There, he studied engineering, mathematics and nuclear physics—all disciplines that would serve him well through later philosophic inquiry. In point of fact, L. Ron Hubbard was the first to rigorously employ Western scientific methods to questions of a spiritual nature. Beyond a basic methodology, however, university offered nothing of what he sought. Indeed, as he later admitted with some vehemence:

*"It was very obvious that I was dealing with and living in a culture which knew less about the mind than the lowest primitive tribe I had ever come in contact with. Knowing also that people in the East were not able to reach as deeply and predictably into the riddles of the mind, as I had been led to expect, I knew I would have to do a lot of research."*

That research consumed the next twenty years. Through the course of it, he would move amongst twenty-one races and cultures, including Pacific Northwest Native American settlements, Philippine Tagalogs and aboriginal people of then remote Caribbean isles. In the simplest terms, his focus lay with two fundamental questions. First, and extending from experimentation conducted at George Washington University, he sought out a long-speculated life force at the root of human consciousness. Next and inextricably linked to the first, he searched for a unifying common denominator of life—a universal yardstick, as it were, with which to determine what was invariably true and workable as regards the human condition.

What amounted to a first philosophic plateau came in 1938 with a now legendary manuscript entitled "Excalibur." In essence it proposed life to be not a random series of chemical reactions, but instead driven by some definable urge underlying all behavior. That urge, he declared, was *Survive!* and it represented the single most pervasive force among all living things. That Man was surviving was not a new idea. That here was the sole common denominator of existence—this was entirely new and therein lay the signpost for all research to follow.

*"That Man was surviving was not a new idea. That here was the sole common denominator of existence—this was entirely new and therein lay the signpost for all research to follow."*

The Second World War proved both an interruption of research and a further impetus: the first owing to service in both the Atlantic and Pacific as a commander of antisubmarine patrols; the second because if anything underscored the need for a workable philosophy to resolve the human condition, it was the unmitigated horror of global conflict. Hence, another summary statement from L. Ron Hubbard at the midpoint of his journey:

*"Man has a madness and it's called war."*

The culmination of research to this juncture came in 1945 at the Oak Knoll Naval Hospital in Oakland, California. Left partially blind from damaged optic nerves and lame with hip and spinal injuries, then

Lieutenant L. Ron Hubbard became one of five thousand servicemen under treatment at Oak Knoll for injuries suffered in combat. Also among them were several hundred former prisoners of internment camps, a significant percentage of whom could not assimilate nutrition and were thus effectively starving. Intrigued by such cases, Mr. Hubbard took it upon himself to administer an early form of Dianetics. In all, fifteen patients received Dianetics counseling to relieve a mental inhibition to recovery. What then ensued and what factually saved the lives of those patients was a discovery of immense ramifications. Namely, and notwithstanding generally held scientific theory, one's state of mind actually took precedence over one's physical condition. That is, our viewpoints, attitudes and overall emotional balance ultimately determined our physical well-being and not the reverse. Or as L. Ron Hubbard himself so succinctly phrased it: *"Function monitored structure."*

Thereafter Mr. Hubbard tested workability on a broad selection of cases drawn from a cross section of American society, circa 1948. Among those case studies were Hollywood performers, industry executives, accident victims from emergency wards and the criminally insane from a Georgia mental institution. In total, he brought Dianetics to bear on more than three hundred individuals before compiling sixteen years of investigation into a manuscript. That work is *Dianetics: The Original Thesis*. Although not initially offered for publication, it nonetheless saw extensive circulation as hectographed manuscripts circulated within scientific/medical circles. Moreover, such was popular response, Mr. Hubbard soon found himself besieged with requests for further information. In eventual reply, he authored what became the all-time bestselling work on the human mind: *Dianetics: The Modern Science of Mental Health*.

Without question, here was a cultural landmark. In what would prove a telling prediction, then national columnist Walter Winchell proclaimed:

*"There is something new coming up in April called Dianetics. A new science which works with the invariability of physical science in the field of the human mind. From all indications it will prove to be as revolutionary for humanity as the first caveman's discovery and utilization of fire."*

If Winchell's statement was bold, it was nonetheless accurate; for with Dianetics came the first definitive explanation of human thinking and behavior. Here, too, was the first means to resolve problems of the human mind, including unreasonable fears, upsets, insecurities and psychosomatic ills of every description.

At the core of such problems lay what Mr. Hubbard termed the *reactive mind* and defined as that "portion of a person's mind which is entirely stimulus-response, which is not under his volitional control and which exerts force and the power of command over his awareness, purposes, thoughts, body and actions." Stored within the reactive mind are *engrams,* defined as mental recordings of pain and unconsciousness. That the mind still recorded perceptions during moments of partial or full unconsciousness was dimly known. But how the engram impacted physiologically, how it acted upon thinking and behavior—this was entirely new. Nor had anyone fathomed the totality of engramic content as contained in the reactive mind and what it spelled in terms of human misery. In short, here lay a mind, as Mr. Hubbard so powerfully phrased it,

*"which makes a man suppress his hopes, which holds his apathies, which gives him irresolution when he should act, and kills him before he has begun to live."*

If ever one wished for incontrovertible proof of Dianetics efficacy, one need only consider what it accomplished. The cases are legion, documented and startling in the extreme: an arthritically paralyzed welder returned to full mobility in a few dozen hours, a legally blind professor regaining sight in under a week and a hysterically crippled housewife returned to normalcy in a single three-hour session. Then there was that ultimate goal of Dianetics processing wherein the reactive mind is vanquished entirely, giving way to the state of Clear with attributes well in advance of anything previously predicted.

Needless to say, as word of *Dianetics* spread, general response was considerable: more than fifty thousand copies sold immediately off the press, while bookstores struggled to keep it on shelves. As evidence of the workability grew—the fact Dianetics actually offered techniques any reasonably intelligent reader could apply—response grew even more dramatic. *"Dianetics—Taking U.S. by Storm"* and *"Fastest Growing Movement in America"* read newspaper headlines through the summer of 1950. While by the end of the year, some wrote of venturing down many highways, along many byroads, into many back alleys of uncertainty and through many strata of life. And

*"...if many before him had roved upon that track, they left no signposts, no road map and revealed but a fraction of what they saw."*

750 Dianetics groups had spontaneously mushroomed from coast to coast and six cities boasted research foundations to help facilitate Mr. Hubbard's advancement of the subject.

That advancement was swift, methodical and at least as revelatory as preceding discoveries. At the heart of what Mr. Hubbard examined through late 1950 and early 1951 lay the most decisive questions of human existence. In an early but telling statement on the matter, he wrote:

*"The further one investigated, the more one came to understand that here, in this creature Homo sapiens, were entirely too many unknowns."*

The ensuing line of research, embarked upon some twenty years earlier, he described as a track of *"knowing how to know."* In a further description of the journey, he metaphorically if many before him had roved upon that track, they left no signposts, no road map and revealed but a fraction of what they saw. Nevertheless, in the early spring of 1952 and through a pivotal lecture in Wichita, Kansas, the result of this search was announced: *Scientology.*

An applied religious philosophy, Scientology represents a statement of human potential that even if echoed in ancient scripture is utterly unparalleled. Among other essential tenets of the Scientology religion: Man is an immortal spiritual being; his experience extends well beyond a single lifetime and his capabilities are unlimited even if not presently realized. In that respect, Scientology represents the ultimate definition of a religion: not just a system of beliefs, but a means of *spiritual transformation.*

How Scientology accomplishes that transformation is through the study of L. Ron Hubbard scriptures and the application of basic terms it may be said that Scientology does not ask one to *strive* toward higher ethical conduct, greater awareness, happiness

*"We are extending to you the precious gift of freedom and immortality—factually, honestly."*

principles therein. The central practice of Scientology is auditing. It is delivered by an auditor, from the Latin *audire,* "to listen." The auditor does not evaluate nor in any way tell one what to think. In short, auditing is not *done* to a person and its benefits can only be achieved through active participation. Indeed, auditing rests on the maxim that only by allowing one to find one's own answer to a problem can that problem be resolved. Precisely to that end, the auditor employs *processes*—precise sets of questions to help one examine otherwise unknown and unwanted sources of travail.

What all this means subjectively is, of course, somewhat ineffable; for by its very definition auditing involves an ascent to states not described in earlier literature. But in very and sanity. Rather, it provides a route to states where all simply *is*—where one becomes more ethical, able, self-determined and happier because that which makes us otherwise is *gone*. While from an all-encompassing perspective and the ultimate ends of auditing, Mr. Hubbard invited those new to Scientology with this:

*"We are extending to you the precious gift of freedom and immortality—factually, honestly."*

The complete route of spiritual advancement is delineated by the Scientology *Bridge*. It presents the precise steps of auditing and training one must walk to realize the full scope of Scientology. Because the Bridge is laid out in a gradient fashion, the advancement is orderly and predictable. If the basic concept is an ancient one—a route across a chasm of ignorance to a higher plateau—what the Bridge presents is altogether new: not some arbitrary sequence of steps, but the most workable means for the recovery of what Mr. Hubbard described as our "immortal, imperishable self, forevermore."

Yet if Scientology represents the route to Man's highest spiritual aspirations, it also means much to his immediate existence—to his family, career and community. That fact is critical to an understanding of the religion and is actually what Scientology is all about: not a doctrine, but the study and handling of the human spirit in relationship to itself, to other life and the universe in which we live. In that respect, L. Ron Hubbard's work embraces *everything*.

"Unless there is a vast alteration in Man's civilization as it stumbles along today," he declared in the mid-1960s, "Man will not be here very long." For signs of that decline, he cited political upheaval, moral putrefaction, violence, racism, illiteracy and drugs. It was in response to these problems, then, that L. Ron Hubbard devoted the better part of his final years. Indeed,

*"Unless there is a vast alteration in Man's civilization as it stumbles along today, Man will not be here very long."*

by the early 1970s his life may be charted directly in terms of his search for solutions to the cultural crises of this modern age.

That he was ultimately successful is borne out in the truly phenomenal growth of Scientology. There are now more than ten thousand groups and organizations in well over 150 nations using the various technologies of Dianetics and Scientology. That his discoveries relating to the human mind and spirit form the basis of all else he accomplished is, in fact, the whole point of this introduction. Thus, what is presented in pages to follow—in the name of better education, crime-free cities, drug-free campuses, stable and ethical organizations and cultural revitalization through the arts—all this and more was derived from discoveries of Dianetics and Scientology. Yet given the sheer scope of accomplishment—as an author, educator, humanitarian, administrator and artist—no such treatment can be entirely complete. For how can one possibly convey, in a few dozen pages, the impact of a life that so deeply touched so many other lives? Nonetheless, this succinct profile of the man and his achievements is provided in the spirit of what he himself declared:

*"If things were a little better known and understood, we would all lead happier lives."*

*"If things were a little better known and understood, we would all lead happier lives."* ■

The materials of Dianetics and Scientology include 3 encyclopedic series and some 3,000 taped lectures. In full, L. Ron Hubbard's philosophic contribution represents more than 75 million written and recorded words. Together these materials constitute the largest single body of work on the human mind and spirit.

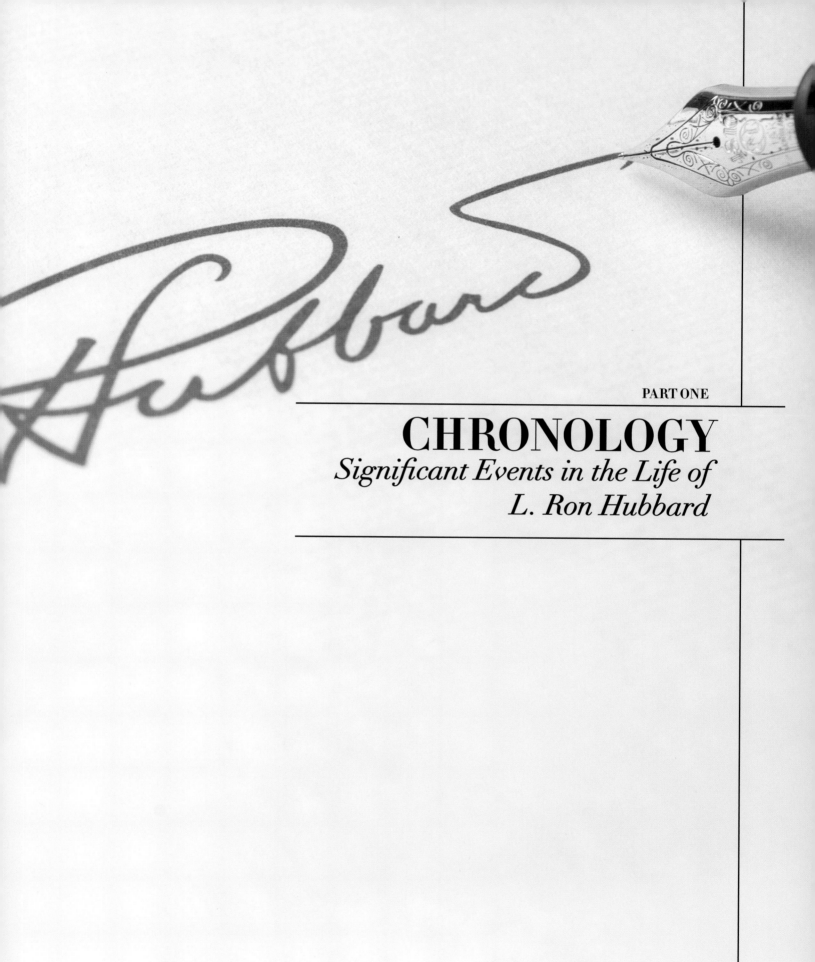

# PART ONE

# CHRONOLOGY
*Significant Events in the Life of*
*L. Ron Hubbard*

# Chronology

## Significant Events in the Life of L. Ron Hubbard

TO WHAT WAS BUT TOUCHED UPON IN PRECEDING PAGES, THE following chronology presents the milestone events along the many avenues L. Ron Hubbard walked—as an adventurer, explorer, author, philosopher and all else that led him to truthfully declare:

*"I have lived no cloistered life*

*and hold in contempt the wise man who has not*

***lived** and the scholar who will not share."*

*"I have seen life from the top down and*

*the bottom up. I know how it looks both ways.*

*And I know there **is** wisdom and*

*that there is hope."*

Kalispell, Montana, 1912

Helena, Montana, 1914

**MARCH 13, 1911** L. Ron Hubbard is born in Tilden, Nebraska, to Harry Ross Hubbard, an officer in the United States Navy and Ledora May Hubbard nee Waterbury.

**1913** The young Ron Hubbard resides with his namesake and maternal grandfather, Lafayette Waterbury, in Kalispell, Montana. Among other adventures from these tender years comes Ron's first memorable encounter with indigenous Blackfeet.

**1914** The extended Waterbury clan, including Ledora May's numerous siblings, relocate to the Montana State capital at Helena. There, Harry Ross secures an outlying ranch affectionately dubbed the "Old Homestead." It borders an immense and imposing landscape that "swallows men up rather easily." Hence, as the adage went, one must live larger than life simply to survive.

1911–1914

A young Ron Hubbard and father en route from
Helena, Montana, to Oakland, California, 1920

Old Tom

**1916–1917** Among other colorful figures in
this still pioneer setting is an outcast Blackfoot
medicine man locally known as Old Tom. A rare
relationship is established as the elderly shaman
imparts tribal lore to a six-year-old Ron Hubbard.
In a ceremony still recalled in Blackfoot legend,
Ron is then ushered into tribal ranks as a blood
brother.

**1916–1917**

USS *Ulysses S. Grant*

**1923** In the wake of his father's promotion to a naval yard at Puget Sound, Ron enters the Boy Scouts. By November 1923, Harry Ross again enjoys promotion and the Hubbard family boards the USS *Ulysses S. Grant* out of San Francisco through a then newly opened Panama Canal to the nation's capital. The voyage proves especially fateful as Ron encounters United States Naval Commander Joseph C. Thompson, recently returned from Vienna and a study of psychoanalysis under Sigmund Freud. For some months thereafter, Thompson walks the twelve-year-old Ron through an informal course of psychoanalytic theory. Although Ron will never embrace psychoanalysis whole cloth, what amounts to a model of the human mind proves unforgettable.

**1924** After earning an impressive array of merit badges, Ron is one of four young men elected to represent scouting at the Presidential Celebration of National Boys' Week. Through the same season, he leads his Washington Troop 10 to victory in regional competition. Whereupon he enters the annals of scouting history as America's youngest Eagle Scout.

**1923–1924**

Guam, 1927

**1927** The now sixteen-year-old L. Ron Hubbard boards the USS *President Madison* outbound from San Francisco to Japan, China and thence to the island of Guam, where his father now serves the naval refueling station. It signals the commencement of an extended Asian sojourn and will leave an indelible impression. While ensconced on Guam, he teaches English in a native school and finds employment in a photographic studio. His own picturesque landscapes and studies of villagers will sell to *National Geographic*. On his return to Helena in early September, he joins the Montana National Guard's 163rd Infantry, distinguishes himself as a marksman and edits the high-school newspaper. But Helena can no longer hold him.

1927

Peking, China, 1928

At the helm of the *Mariana Maru*,
China Seas, 1928

*Mariana Maru,* inter-island schooner, 1928

**1928–1929** Impetuously boarding the USS *Henderson* out of San Diego, the now seventeen-year-old L. Ron Hubbard again ventures eastward. Upon landing at Guam (much to his father's surprise), he signs on as helmsman and supercargo with a twin-masted schooner bound for the China coast. Through the next fourteen months, as he himself would later phrase it, he drinks deep from the "airy spiralings and dread mysteries" of Asia; and while abiding questions remain unanswered, his path of research and discovery is now evident.

Washington, DC, 1930

**1930–1931** Matriculates to George Washington University, where he studies engineering and molecular physics. But what most engages him is extracurricular experimentation to isolate a long-postulated life force at the root of human consciousness. He is further searching out a long-pondered Dynamic Principle of Existence for the unification of all available knowledge. Also in an extracurricular vein he earns national renown as a free-flight daredevil and Midwest barnstormer.

It is additionally through these collegiate years, he embarks on a literary career supplying aviation articles for *The Sportsman Pilot,* short stories for the university literary review and an award-winning one-act play entitled *The God Smiles.* Finally, and no less significantly, he serves as a freelance reporter-photographer for the *Washington Herald,* while performing as a balladeer on Washington radio WOL. (Hereafter both photography and music will prove lifelong pursuits.)

**1930–1931**

*Doris Hamlin,* of the 1932 Caribbean
Motion Picture Expedition

**1932–1933** Organizes and helms the Caribbean
Motion Picture Expedition. It is a 5,000-mile
voyage aboard a last four-masted schooner.
Expeditionary aims include filming newsreel
footage of Caribbean pirate haunts. The expedition
further yields floral and reptile specimens for the
University of Michigan and photographs for the
*New York Times.*

**1932–1933**

Puerto Rico, 1932

Upon completion of the voyage, he embarks on the West Indies Mineralogical Expedition and so completes the first mineralogical survey of Puerto Rico under American protectorship. (See the L. Ron Hubbard Series edition, *Adventurer/Explorer: Daring Deeds & Unknown Realms.*)

**1932–1933**

L. Ron Hubbard, center second row, president of the American Fiction Guild's New York chapter, 1936

Washington State, 1935

**1934–1936** Publishes a first tale of intrigue for what was then a literary phenomenon: *Pulp Fiction*. Thereafter, while averaging a similarly phenomenal 70,000 words a month, he swiftly assumes legendary status as an author of mysteries, westerns, aerial thrillers, high-seas adventure and even the occasional romance. In accord with his stature, and notwithstanding his relative youth, he is elected president of American Fiction Guild's New York chapter. In such capacity, he now joins a society of authors comprising a veritable pantheon of Pulp Fiction Kings, including: Raymond Chandler, Dashiell Hammett, Edgar Rice Burroughs and H. P. Lovecraft. Thereafter, he divides his time between New York City and a writer's retreat in Port Orchard, Washington.

1934–1936

**1937** Such is L. Ron Hubbard's popularity that Columbia Pictures purchases film rights for an LRH novelette entitled *Murder at Pirate Castle.* The author is enlisted to adapt his tale for the screen as an episodic serial. Retitled *The Secret of Treasure* *Island,* it breaks all box office records of the day and L. Ron Hubbard is next enlisted to coscript *The Mysterious Pilot, The Great Adventures of Wild Bill Hickok* and *The Spider Returns.*

Writer's retreat, Port Orchard, Washington

On his return to Port Orchard from Hollywood in the autumn of 1937, he designs a series of laboratory experiments to examine cellular memory—specifically inherited memory traces passed from one generation to the next. Albeit years hence, this is the kernel discovery of the engram and the springboard to that long-sought Dynamic Principle of Existence, *Survive!* It also provides the ideological foundation for a first philosophic work: a now legendary manuscript entitled "Excalibur."

**1937**

The Alaskan Radio Experimental Expedition, 1940

**1938** At a pivotal juncture in pulp fiction history, L. Ron Hubbard is enjoined by publishing magnate Street & Smith to author tales for *Astounding Science Fiction*. In particular, he is to infuse an overly machine-driven genre with a human element. The result is a profound change in literary direction and a Golden Age of Science Fiction dawns.

**1939–1940** Whilst authoring such classic tales as *Death's Deputy, Fear* and *Final Blackout,* L. Ron Hubbard embarks on the Alaskan Radio Experimental Expedition. Conducted under the auspices of the Explorers Club, where he was admitted as an active member in February 1940, the five-month voyage of 1,500 miles courses through a treacherous Inside Passage from Puget Sound to Ketchikan, Alaska.

En route Captain L. Ron Hubbard annotates charts for the United States Hydrographic Office and tests a prototypic radio navigation system that significantly bears upon the development of LORAN (LOng RAnge Navigation). He additionally examines indigenous native culture, principally the Tlingit, Haidas and Aleutian islanders. On 17th of December 1940, the United States Bureau of Marine Inspection and Navigation awards L. Ron Hubbard a Master of Steam and Motor Vessels license. (See the L. Ron Hubbard Series edition, *Master Mariner: At the Helm Across Seven Seas.*)

**1940**

US Navy subchaser under L. Ron Hubbard
command, North Pacific, 1943

**1941–1945** On 29th of March 1941, L. Ron Hubbard earns his Master of Sail Vessels license for Any Ocean. Three months later, he is commissioned as Lieutenant (jg) of the United States Navy Reserve. With United States involvement in the Second World War, Lieutenant Hubbard is dispatched to Australia, where he coordinates relief for beleaguered forces under General Douglas MacArthur. Upon his return to American soil in March 1942, he assumes command of a convoy escort vessel in the Atlantic, then a subchaser in the Pacific. He additionally serves as a naval instructor and chief navigation officer. In anticipation of service with Allied occupational forces, he is elected to the United States Naval School of Military Government at Princeton University.

In early 1945, while recovering at Oak Knoll Naval Hospital from injuries sustained in combat, he employs the first techniques of Dianetics to dramatic effect: speeding recovery of otherwise terminal patients. With this demonstrative advance, he is now dedicated to the refinement and testing of Dianetics in application.

Los Angeles, California, 1948

**1946–1949** Upon discharge from the navy in February 1946, so begins intense but methodical Dianetics refinement. In his capacity as a lay practitioner, he ultimately addresses some 350 cases drawn from matrimonial bureaus, convalescent homes, probation departments, a Georgia State orphanage and mental wards. As a Special Officer with the Los Angeles Police Department, he further studies the criminal element.

With case material amassed, he compiles results from a sixteen-year investigation into a summary manuscript. That work is *Dianetics: The Original Thesis*. While initially unpublished, the manuscript broadly circulates within medical/scientific circles. Response is such that he is urged by associates to author a definitive text on the subject. In late 1949, the first formally published announcement of Dianetics appears in *The Explorers Journal*. It is appropriately titled *Terra Incognita: The Mind*.

**1950** Under contract with Hermitage House Publishing, L. Ron Hubbard's *Dianetics: The Modern Science of Mental Health* is completed in February. Immediately thereafter, he authors *Dianetics: The Evolution of a Science* for a popular magazine. On May 9, 1950, *Dianetics: The Modern Science of Mental Health* is released and soon hits the *New York Times* bestseller list. It remains on that list for twenty-eight consecutive weeks and inspires what newspapers describe as the fastest-growing movement in America.

To both advance the subject technically and meet demands for formal instruction, a first Hubbard Dianetic Research Foundation is formed in Elizabeth, New Jersey. Sister organizations soon follow suit in New York, Chicago and Los Angeles. By the end of December, L. Ron Hubbard has delivered more than 140 lectures, including a now legendary address to an audience of six thousand at the Los Angeles Shrine Auditorium.

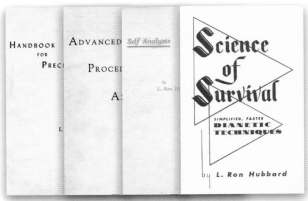

**1951** As anticipated in the final pages of *Dianetics,* L. Ron Hubbard embarks on a trail of research to isolate that long-pondered *life force* and what he describes as a "higher echelon of universal origin and destination." He is also engaged in a refinement of Dianetics technology for swifter methods of approach and result. This developmental trail is recorded in 112 lectures and his authored works of 1951, including: *Science of Survival, Advanced Procedure and Axioms, Self Analysis* and *Handbook for Preclears.* To consolidate the administration and advancement of Dianetics, he further forms a first Hubbard College in Wichita, Kansas.

**1951**

Auditing demonstration

Hubbard Association of Scientologists, Phoenix, Arizona

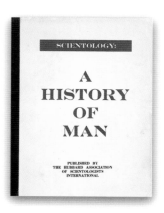

**1952** Having determined a human being to be fundamentally spiritual, so begins a track of inquiry to determine the fundamental truths of spiritual existence. What ultimately and inevitably follows is the founding of Scientology. While it is initially announced at the Hubbard College in Wichita, Kansas, the first Hubbard Association of Scientologists forms in Phoenix, Arizona, with an international arm in London, England. His path of advancement is recorded in 182 lectures and a landmark work entitled *Scientology: A History of Man*. It is also at this juncture that L. Ron Hubbard becomes the first to accomplish a separation of the human spirit from the body along scientific lines (rather than mere belief), at which point the fact of immortality becomes incontrovertible.

1952

**1953–1954** As the announcement of Scientology immediately inspires worldwide attention, Mr. Hubbard answers requests for lectures and instruction in London. He further tours the Continent presenting Scientology to religious and academic communities in France, Germany and Spain.

1953–1954

Through simultaneous technical advancement, he now very literally measures the electronics of human thought and the inherent potential of the human spirit. On his return to Phoenix, in the spring of 1954 he authors *The Creation of Human Ability*. The preceding discoveries coupled with what is presented through the pages of that work effectively comprise the core of the Scientology religion.

Founding Church of Scientology Washington, DC

**1955** With respect to the meteoric growth of Scientology, L. Ron Hubbard relocates from Phoenix to the nation's capital and there forms the Founding Church of Washington, DC. In addition to his continued technical advancement of the subject, he now serves as Scientology's first Executive Director. In such capacity, he authors an initial body of organizational policy, comprising a technology all unto itself and perfectly mirroring central truths of Scientology as applied to group endeavor.

**1955**

An L. Ron Hubbard lecture from a series
entitled "Nuclear Radiation and Health"

**1956–1958** *"Scientology does not teach you. It only reminds you. For the information was yours in the first place."* Thus, L. Ron Hubbard presents Scientology fundamentals with *Scientology: The Fundamentals of Thought* and thus he brings Scientology to bear on the fundamental predicament of modern existence. Included in the offing is a landmark series of lectures on radioactive fallout and a then omnipresent threat of nuclear holocaust. He is the first to decry the hydrogen bomb as not a weapon per se, but an instrument of terror to engender mass hysteria. So compelling is the argument it inspires commensurate debates in British Parliament.

**1956–1958**

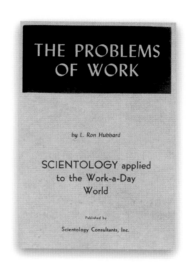

Also from the era is Scientology applied to the workaday world as presented in L. Ron Hubbard's *The Problems of Work*. It is another presentation of Scientology fundamentals. In this case, the technology to empower working people under an aphorism that reads: *"They are not cogs in a mighty machine. They are the machine itself."* Finally and simultaneous to all the above and more, he steers Scientology from Europe and America, while "commuting" between Washington and London to deliver more than three hundred lectures.

Saint Hill Manor, East Grinstead, England

**1959–1961** To provide a worldwide emanation point for Scientology training and dissemination, he purchases Saint Hill Manor on the East Grinstead downs in Sussex, England. The 55-acre luxury estate is the former residence of the Maharajah of Jaipur, but will ever after remain L. Ron Hubbard's home.

Welcoming Scientologists to his new home at Saint Hill Manor

**1959–1961**

Moreover, the estate soon gains international renown as the site of L. Ron Hubbard's landmark horticultural experimentation wherein he categorically demonstrates plants emit emotional wavelengths paralleling other life forms. (See the L. Ron Hubbard Series edition, *Horticulture: For a Greener World.*)

**1959–1961**

Saint Hill Manor office

HUBBARD ASSOCIATION OF SCIENTOLOGISTS INTERNATIONAL

WITH OFFICES IN... JOHANNESBURG, WASHINGTON, MELBOURNE, NEW YORK, LONDON, LOS ANGELES, SYDNEY, AUCKLAND, PARIS & BERLIN...

Johannesburg, South Africa

It is also at this juncture he embarks on a round-the-world flight to Australia for a now famed series of lectures in Melbourne. He further ventures to South Africa for an equally famed series of lectures in Johannesburg. In this way, he extends Scientology across the Southern Hemisphere.

Finally, and of most lasting significance, he inaugurates the *Saint Hill Special Briefing Course* as Scientology's single most comprehensive training program. In full, the Briefing Course will present the entire history of technical development and students will ultimately follow L. Ron Hubbard's footsteps to the state of Clear and beyond.

**1959–1961**

**1962–1964** Scientology technical advancement is unceasing as faithfully recorded in lectures to Briefing Course students. In a word, Mr. Hubbard is now mapping the Scientology Bridge to never previously envisioned heights of awareness and ability. He is additionally now developing a universal pattern of organization paralleling axiomatic Scientology truths bearing upon survival and prosperity. Then, too, this is the era wherein he isolates primary barriers to learning and literacy. The result is Study Technology, now employed globally in both Scientology organizations and secular education. Finally, he further resumes his photographic pursuits with award-winning English landscapes exhibited in Continental galleries.

**1965** In a culminating moment of Scientology history, Mr. Hubbard unveils the *Classification and Gradation Chart*. Delineating the step-by-step advancement to ever-higher states of awareness and ability, this is that long-sought Scientology *Bridge*. Almost immediately thereafter, and born from a parallel track of research, he unveils the *Seven Division Scientology Organizing Board*. This, then, is that universal pattern of successful operation for any group endeavor.

**1965**

*Enchanter* embarking on the Hubbard Geological Survey Expedition

**1966–1967** Departing Saint Hill to secure a base for advanced Scientology research, Mr. Hubbard ventures to Rhodesia. There, he works to extend basic human rights to native Africans and is, in fact, still remembered as a "rare voice in the land." Upon his return to England, he delivers the final lectures of the Saint Hill Special Briefing Course; whereupon he accepts an Explorers Club flag for the Hubbard Geological Survey Expedition. It is designated to examine ancient Mediterranean civilizations and so amplify Man's knowledge of history. It is manned by an elite body of Scientologists comprising the first of the Sea Organization and thereafter dedicated to supporting LRH research and advancing Scientology as a whole.

The venture launches in early 1967 aboard two expeditionary vessels, *Enchanter* (later rechristened *Diana*) and *Avon River* (latterly *Athena*). What ensues is a revolutionary explanation of why civilizations collapse and the singular factor behind all human conflict. In November 1967, he accepts delivery of the 3,200-ton *Royal Scotman* (latterly *Apollo*). She will serve as Mr. Hubbard's home and research vessel for the next eight years.

The *Apollo*

**1968–1970** While simultaneously mapping upper spans of the Scientology Bridge and standardizing Scientology application, Mr. Hubbard now addresses bedrock failings of society at large. Initially and in particular, he examines precipitating factors of drug addiction. What ensues is a Scientology regimen to address underlying *causes* of usage. Also through these years comes his advancement of Study Technology to address downtrending literacy rates and another regimen entirely for humane criminal rehabilitation. While beyond even that, he authors an entire series of articles on cultural degradation. (See the L. Ron Hubbard Series edition, *Freedom Fighter: Articles & Essays.*)

**1971–1973** Having standardized a pattern of organizational form and function, Mr. Hubbard now addresses the exigencies of managing an international network of organizations. To that end, he isolates workable principles of personnel utilization, target attainment, executive performance, financial management, data analysis and more. These principles are found in *The Management Series* and are employed far beyond Scientology organizations.

Through what remains of 1972 and well into 1973, Mr. Hubbard conducts a sociological study in and around New York City. He is now working to isolate root causes of late twentieth-century cultural decline and from these studies comes an array of programs for social betterment. He additionally examines deleterious trends in the modern diet, which later prove significant in addressing residual effects of drugs.

1968–1973

Curaçao, 1975

**1974–1975** Upon completing a transatlantic crossing in October of 1974, the *Apollo* lands in the Lesser Antilles. There, Mr. Hubbard lends his considerable photographic talents to the Curaçao Tourist Board. In the same vein, he further photographs Curaçao's Mikvé Israel–Emanuel Synagogue (the oldest Jewish house of worship in the Americas and still presenting L. Ron Hubbard photographs in synagogue guidebooks). Finally, and all but concurrently, he conducts an extensive photographic shoot for Scientology publications.

In no way, however, are such pursuits the extent of his artistic endeavor; for having organized a music and dance troupe to entertain at ports of call, these years also see his codification of artistic presentation, composition, arranging and recording.

By mid-1975, activities aboard the *Apollo* outstrip the vessel's capacity and Mr. Hubbard returns to the United States. He initially settles in Dunedin, Florida, where he produces/records local church choirs of every denomination for radio performance and a rejuvenation of regional religious influence.

L. Ron Hubbard's desert estate in La Quinta, California

**1976–1980** Relocating to a Southern California desert ranch in La Quinta, he organizes, trains and supervises a film production unit. Through the next five years, he will script, shoot, direct and produce an array of Scientology instructional films. No less intensively, he further now examines residual effects of substance abuse and specifically the fact drug traces remain in the body even years after ingestion. Accordingly, he develops the Purification Program. Coupled with his 1969 discoveries, his development of an LRH drug rehabilitation regimen is now complete and proves the single most effective regimen in the rehab arena. Finally, and likewise bearing upon the course of generations, he again addresses inadequacies of education and spiraling illiteracy. What ensues are discoveries now at work in L. Ron Hubbard's Key to Life, and which indeed proves a revolution in learning.

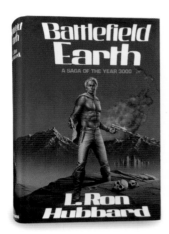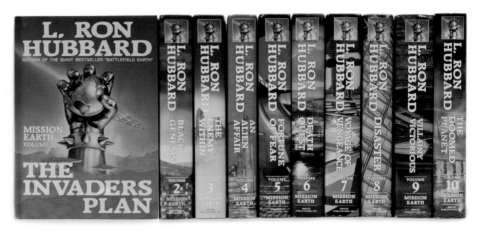

**1981–1983** *"Trying to survive in a chaotic, dishonest and generally immoral society is difficult."* Thus L. Ron Hubbard introduces *The Way to Happiness* and thus he presents society at large with a first nonreligious moral code and common sense guide to living. Initial distribution promulgates a grass-roots movement, particularly within business communities and law enforcement.

Subsequently and in celebration of his fiftieth anniversary as a professional writer, he authors *Battlefield Earth: A Saga of the Year 3000*.

It immediately garners international acclaim and worldwide bestseller status. What is generally regarded as his magnum opus, however, is the ten-volume *Mission Earth* series and which, all told, makes for an output of some two million words through these years. Moreover, Mr. Hubbard will soon complement both works with first-ever soundtracks to novels: the highly innovative *Space Jazz* for *Battlefield Earth* and the critically acclaimed *Mission Earth* album.

**1981–1983**

L. Ron Hubbard's rolling hills estate in Creston, California

**1984–1986** *"And what is one rising to, after all? One is rising to eternity."* From just such a vantage point, and while residing at a central California estate, L. Ron Hubbard now indeed advances Scientology into realms that touch eternity. Meanwhile, the *Mission Earth* series is now published and the successive appearance of each volume on the *New York Times* bestseller list will long be remembered as a landmark event in publishing history. Mr. Hubbard further writes and scores still another album, *The Road to Freedom* as a musical statement of fundamental Scientology principles.

**1984–1986**

**JANUARY 24, 1986** Mr. Hubbard departs this life, having achieved all he set out to accomplish. His global impact, however, soon to be measured in the tens of millions, continues to grow.

In reply to demands for his literary works, all earlier titles are republished. The first, *Final Blackout* and *Fear,* promptly ride bestseller lists, repeating popularity from fifty years earlier. In full, forty L. Ron Hubbard works appear on international bestseller lists. Moreover, with combined sales of fiction and nonfiction titles, he becomes the most published and translated author in history, as recorded in the *Guinness Book of Records.*

Similarly, as Scientology is the only major religion born in the twentieth century, there is no other religious founder in modern history with such broadly popular appeal. Hence, the ten thousand Scientology churches, missions and related organizations spanning every continent today.

The appeal of Mr. Hubbard's secular works is likewise unprecedented, as exemplified by the fact all his technologies have since inspired global movements:

- Study Technology now employed across entire school systems at the behest of federal governments.
- His technology for drug rehabilitation now in some fifty nations and truthfully credited with the salvation of at least a million terminal addicts.
- His program for criminal reform now likewise international and just as truthfully credited with reducing 70 and 80 percent recidivism to negligible fractions.
- *The Way to Happiness* distributed by the millions across notoriously violent lands; whereupon national crime rates precipitously plummet to levels not seen in decades.

- And the hundreds of thousands of organizations in well over a hundred nations now employing L. Ron Hubbard's technology for survival and prosperity.

Meanwhile, in recognition of a man who unquestionably stands as the world's single most influential author, educator, humanitarian and philosopher, some four hundred United States mayors and governors proclaim March 13 "L. Ron Hubbard Day" and May 9 "Dianetics Day."

Moreover, with continued dissemination of L. Ron Hubbard's work, his impact on lives triples every decade—all towards the fulfillment of his dream for:

*"A civilization without insanity, without criminals and without war, where the able can prosper and honest beings can have rights, and where Man is free to rise to greater heights."*

Today, many millions embrace L. Ron Hubbard's legacy to uplift their lives, their communities and Mankind as a whole. To provide for those newly discovering that legacy, new organizations are continually arising and there is now no major city on Earth that does not offer the fruit of his discoveries according to the spirit in which it was given:

*"I know no man who has any monopoly upon the wisdom of this universe. It belongs to those who can use it to help themselves and others.*

*"If things were a little better known and understood, we would all lead happier lives.*

*"And there is a way to know them and there is a way to freedom.*

*"The old must give way to the new, falsehood must become exposed by truth, and truth, though fought, always in the end prevails."*

---

**1986**

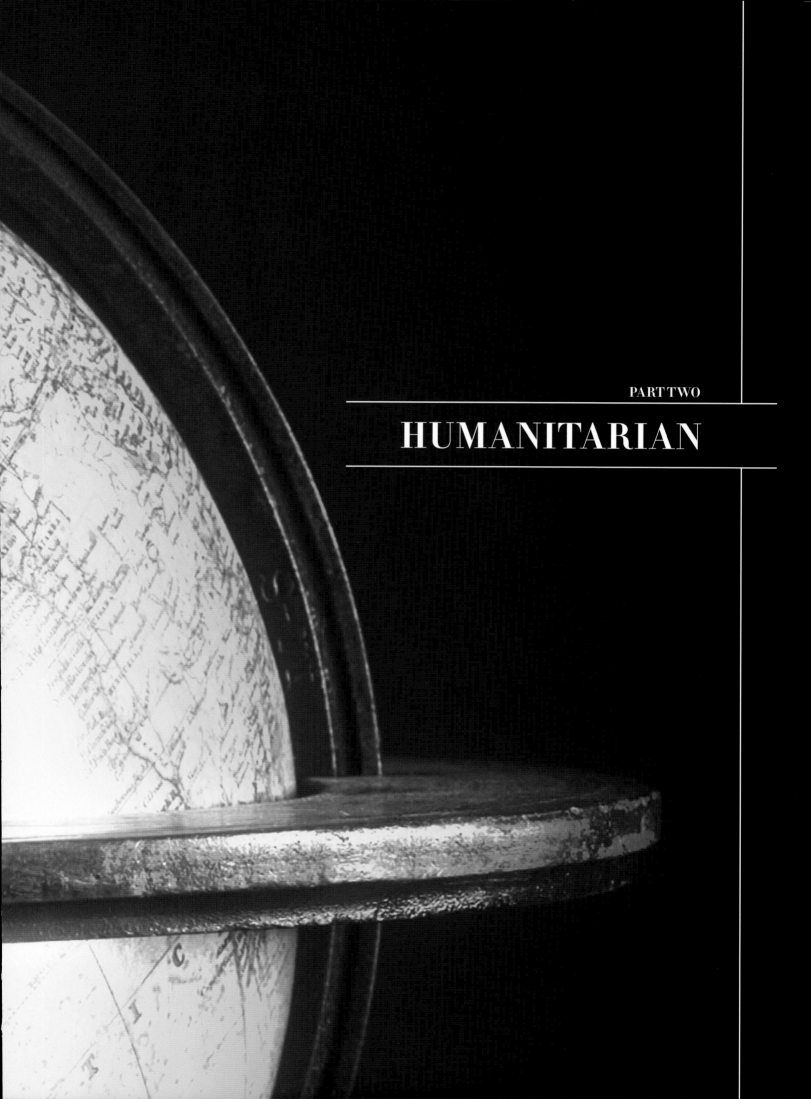

# PART TWO

# HUMANITARIAN

# Humanitarian

NOTWITHSTANDING THIS CENTURY'S ARRAY OF technological wonders—in medicine, transportation, nuclear energy and electronic communications—we live in a seriously troubled society. Under the triple onslaught of drug abuse, criminality and declining morals much of this world has truly become a

wasteland. By some estimates, marijuana, for example, has become the largest cash crop in America, while illegal drugs gross estimated annual revenues of some $500 billion. Added to these figures are another $700-plus billion spent on medical and psychiatric drugs—until, at last, we are faced with a crisis of truly planetary proportions wherein the people of Earth spend more money on drugs than most nations produce in terms of goods and services.

Yet ill-gotten revenue is only one measure of today's drug abuse toll. The link with crime is another. According to United States Justice Department studies, half of all those arrested for violent crimes test positive for illegal drugs, which in turn translates into well over a million acts of violence a year...and the cost of *that* in terms of human misery is incalculable.

At the arguable bottom of both drug abuse and criminality lies what has been termed "a postmodern moral crisis." Here, too, the facts are disturbing: More than 40 percent of all marriages end in divorce; another 40 percent of all American youth readily admit they lie for financial gain, and still another 64 percent admit to cheating on exams. The picture grows grimmer still in light of cyberspace iniquity. To wit: at least 10 percent of all websites qualify as pornographic while some 40 percent of all business software is pirated. It is not surprising, then, that as rates of burglary, embezzlement and all other varieties of larceny assume epidemic proportions, historians have come to view this era as an age of moral inequity unrivaled since the fall of Rome.

Sensing where this world was headed as early as 1950, L. Ron Hubbard began to search out a means by which, as he wrote:

*"Man again can find his own feet, can find himself in a very confused, mechanistic society and can recover to himself some of the happiness, some of the sincerity and some of the love and kindness with which he was created."*

Thus comes his humanitarian technologies to reclaim human decency and thus all you will discover in pages to follow. ∎

The **BASIC STUDY** Manual

Based on the works of
**L. RON HUBBARD**

Based on the works of
**L. RON HUBBARD**

Based on the works of
**L. RON HUBBARD**

Based on the works of
**L. RON HUBBARD**

## Solutions to
# Education

"TODAY'S CHILDREN WILL BECOME TOMORROW'S CIVILIZATION."

—LRH

As early as 1950, L. Ron Hubbard warned that any lapse in the quality of education would severely impact on the quality of life. In particular and most incisively:

*"The end and goal of any society, as it addresses the problem of education, is to raise the ability, the initiative and the cultural level and, with all these, the survival level of that society. And when a society forgets any one of these things, it is destroying itself by its own educational mediums."*

Decades later, Mr. Hubbard's observation has proven nightmarishly accurate and continued disintegration of social infrastructures may well prove inevitable unless the deterioration of educational systems is arrested. To cite but a few disturbing facts: over 45 percent of all students leaving or graduating high school lack necessary reading and writing skills intrinsic to daily living; the American high-school dropout rate hovers at approximately 30 percent across inner-city areas; while according to the president of a teachers' association, up to 50 percent of all new instructors quit the profession within the first five years, in part owing to implied threats of bodily harm; and Scholastic Aptitude Test scores of American students have sunk to levels considerably lower than those achieved by students just a few decades earlier.

Elsewhere across the Western world, the numbers are scarcely more encouraging. A British government study reported that a quarter of the English workforce is unable to add the menu prices of a hamburger, French fries, apple pie and coffee. Moreover, one out of five British students could not correctly locate Great Britain on a world map. All told, these dismal figures translate into a depressing economic scenario with annual costs to businesses in lost production and re-education now touching the $250 billion mark. Moreover, when one factors in the grim links between illiteracy and criminality, world educational failures become too bleak to tally. ∎

# Study Technology

IT IS INTO THE FACE OF A POSTMODERN academic crisis that L. Ron Hubbard presented his educational methods. Drawn from some four decades of experience as an educator, these methods represent the first comprehensive understanding of the actual barriers to effective learning. Mr. Hubbard further developed a precise technology to overcome those barriers and thus how to learn and apply *any* body of knowledge.

In total, his contribution to the field is known as *Study Technology* and provides the first fully workable approach to teaching students *how* to learn. It offers methods for recognizing and resolving all difficulties in absorbing material, including a previously unacknowledged barrier that ultimately lies at the root of all failures to pursue a given course of study. In short, then, Study Technology allows *anyone* to learn *anything*.

Because it is based on fundamentals common to everyone, it further cuts across all socioeconomic and cultural boundaries. Moreover, it achieves uniformly consistent results with *all* age groups. Indeed, the three definitive texts on the subject, *The Basic Study Manual, Study Skills for Life* and *Learning How to Learn* essentially differ only in their treatment of the material. The first is designed

for teenagers and above, while the second is aimed at younger readers, with the third offering the basics of Study Technology to children between the ages of eight and twelve.

The point being: Mr. Hubbard's technology for learning and literacy is no less effective in elementary schools than it is in high schools, trade schools and universities, not to mention executive suites of multinational corporations. Furthermore, end results are uniform from one arena to the next inasmuch as the three barriers to comprehension are identical from one learner to another.

To wit and in brief: the first barrier to study, Mr. Hubbard describes as an *absence of mass* and defines it in terms of a physiological response to learning when the physical object one is studying is absent. Thus, for example, if one were attempting to grasp the operation of a tractor without an actual tractor present or reasonable facsimile thereof (an illustration or model), one would suffer various adverse reactions, including, but not limited to, headaches and dizziness.

The second barrier to study, he describes as *too steep a gradient* and defines in terms of attempting to

# The First Barrier to Study

*absence of mass or physical object one is studying*

# The Second Barrier to Study

*too steep a study gradient*

# The Third Barrier to Study

*all becomes distinctly blank beyond a word
not understood or wrongly understood*

*"The end and goal of any society, as it addresses the problem of education, is to raise the ability, the initiative and the cultural level and, with all these, the survival level of that society. And when a society forgets any one of these things, it is destroying itself by its own educational mediums."*

—*L. Ron Hubbard*

master a particular datum or skill without grasping the necessary previous step. By way of example, he points to the student driver unable to coordinate hands and feet to manually shift gears. Although one might imagine the difficulty lay with complications of shifting, in fact there is some *earlier* noncomprehended or unmastered skill, perhaps simply keeping the vehicle on the road.

The third and most important barrier is the *misunderstood word,* which he explains in this wise: *Have you ever read to the bottom of a page only to realize you cannot recall anything on that page?* Therein lies the phenomena of the misunderstood word, i.e., everything is distinctly blank beyond a word not understood or wrongly understood. Conversely, when the troublesome word is pinpointed and properly defined, all becomes miraculously clear. The misunderstood word leads to a vast array of adverse mental effects and significantly bears upon education as a whole, not to mention the whole of the human learning process. In that respect, it is the root problem behind all inabilities and all failures in education.

To rectify the problem Mr. Hubbard developed *Word Clearing.* It comprises a complete technology for addressing misunderstood words and is properly defined as "the subject and action of clearing away the ignorance, misunderstoods and false definitions of words and the barriers to their use." Moreover, when taking into account the totality of his methods for surmounting the Three Barriers to Study—*that* is Study Technology and therein lies all one need know to assimilate any subject or master any skill. ∎

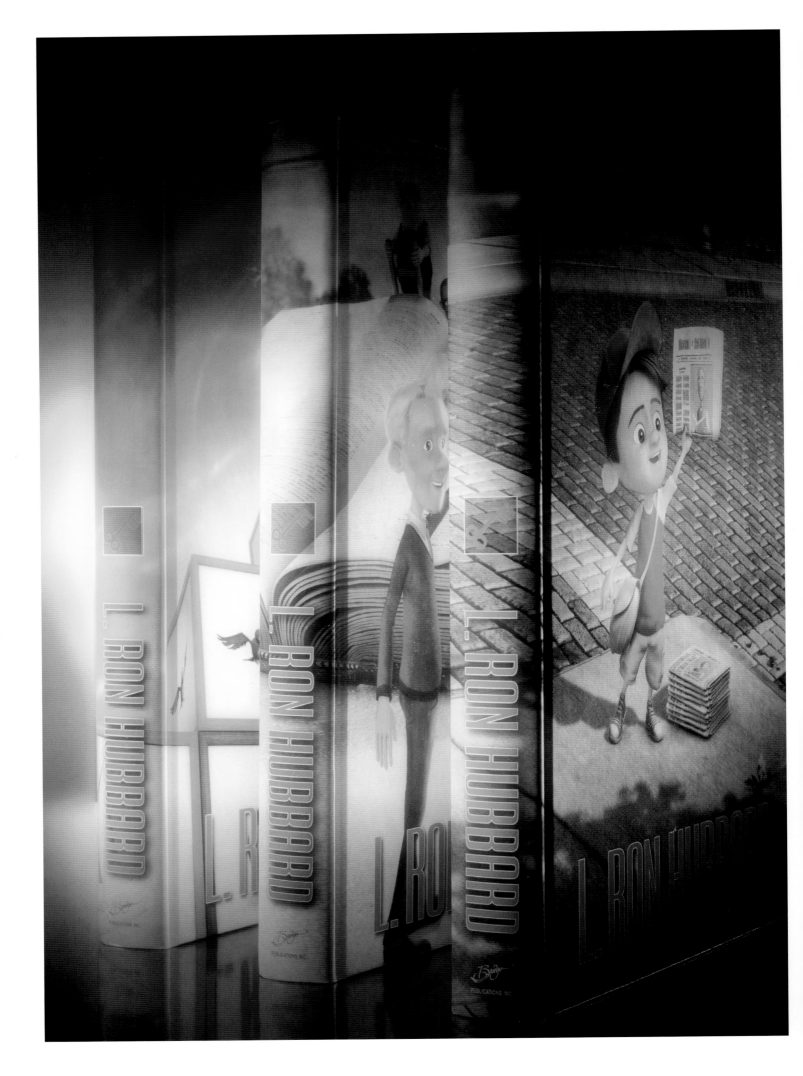

# Key to Life

HOWEVER REVELATORY IS L. RON Hubbard's Study Technology, no discussion of his educational contribution is replete without mention of his *Key to Life Course*. His developmental trail to Key to Life says much about both Mr. Hubbard's approach to problems and the greater educational decline through the 1960s and 1970s.

As he rightly pointed out, three cultural factors through the latter decades of the twentieth century combined to seriously diminish our ability to communicate. First, general education standards fell as new systems ignored fundamentals of reading, writing and grammar. That decline, in turn, was hastened with the advent of television and more particularly mothers who plunked down their children in front of TVs to let a continuous inflow of images serve as both leash and baby sitter. Finally, and particularly through the 1960s, came the drug scourge to further dull the minds of a television generation. In consequence, whole generations were no longer able to comprehend or convey information. Moreover—and herein lay Mr. Hubbard's entrance to the problem—those classes of the '60s and '70s were unable to utilize his earlier educational tools, simply because they lacked a comprehension of the basic structure of

language itself. Needless to say, the problem has only been exacerbated with the advent of wireless communication, reducing language to monosyllabic slang. It was not for nothing, then, that Mr. Hubbard so rightly envisioned entire generations *"out of communication."*

But if one truly comprehended what one read and heard and if one were to make oneself comprehended by others, all life would gloriously open. On the other hand, to the degree one cannot express oneself or make oneself understood by others, life becomes eclipsed. Such is the subject of the Key to Life Course. Step by step, it literally strips away reasons why one cannot clearly comprehend what one reads, writes and hears and why one is not comprehended by others.

Central to the course is a view of language, not as a random conglomeration of words arranged by grammarians, but a means to facilitate the communication of ideas. It holds words not as sacred symbols to be dissected and classified for their own sake, but as tools for use. Likewise, Mr. Hubbard presents an entirely new view of English grammar, not as a study of rules, but as the way in which words are organized

*"If grammar is defined as the way words are organized into speech and writings so as to convey exact thoughts, ideas and meanings among people, students will be eager to study it.*

*"Grammar is something people need in order to understand and to be understood and that is the end of it."*

—*L. Ron Hubbard*

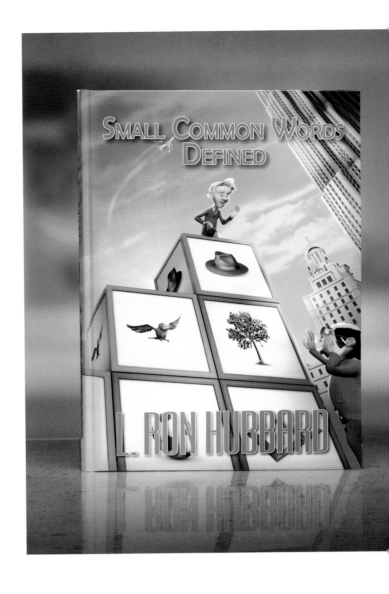

so as to precisely convey thoughts and ideas amongst people.

Accordingly, his statement on the subject is aptly entitled *The New Grammar*. By way of background, he points out that if the man in the street has no clear concept of grammar, it is because the subject is traditionally unclear. Indeed, in the hands of grammarians, with their intricately diagramed sentences, the subject has become nothing if not authoritarian. Then, too, the subject was so wholly opinionated that he could not find a standard text that did not contradict other texts.

Thus he presented *The New Grammar*. It not only presents a new explanation of grammar, it also completely redefines the subject for everyday use. In that respect, Mr. Hubbard has

done nothing less than take English grammar away from "authorities" and return it to everyday people. To that end, he has stripped the subject of its arbitraries, contradictions and all that simply has no point. In its place, he presents easily comprehended essentials of the language as it is used and to facilitate its use.

To that same end, he has even supplied illustrations to convey what students might normally fail to grasp with only the written word. In fact, all Key to Life materials are so illustrated, for as Mr. Hubbard reasoned: how else can one teach the meaning of a word to a student who does not understand the words used to teach him? Thus *The New Grammar* and other Key to Life texts define all concepts with *pictures*.

The result is a work that masterfully clarifies the construction of English in order to facilitate and enhance communication. As Associate Professor of Philosophy of Language at American University, Washington, DC, David Rodier, declared, "This book takes grammar and makes it easy. It helps individuals to understand the basic building blocks of the English language and how to use those building blocks to better communicate, express their thoughts and understand what they read. Only a professional writer with a writer's sensitivity to language could have written such an innovative approach to grammar. Only such a writer would see grammar not as full of constricting rules, but full of possibilities for rich expressions of thought and action." In that

respect, he concludes, "This is a brilliant book by a brilliant mind. In fact, it is a revolution in thought."

No less may be said for Mr. Hubbard's second key text, *Small Common Words Defined*. Again, the work reflects a distillation of the language into its fundamental units. The text also reflects his critical discovery that the primary stumbling block to understanding a sentence is not the long and obscure word, but the simple words, e.g., "to," "the," "an." If the point seems minor, it is not; for although one may be able to read and pronounce the sentence "good as gold," few can actually define the word "as," and thus lack *full* comprehension. To further appreciate the problem, one need only open a standard dictionary and examine the various definitions

*"This book takes grammar and makes it easy. It helps individuals to understand the basic building blocks of the English language and how to use those building blocks to better communicate, express their thoughts and understand what they read. Only a professional writer with a writer's sensitivity to language could have written such an innovative approach to grammar. Only such a writer would see grammar not as full of constricting rules, but full of possibilities for rich expressions of thought and action. This is a brilliant book by a brilliant mind. In fact, it is a revolution in thought."*

*—David Rodier, Associate Professor of Philosophy of Language, American University, Washington, DC*

for that word. The grammarian may be satisfied, but the average reader is not—as borne out by Mr. Hubbard's late 1970s study among college graduates who could not define even the simplest

phonetic codes, punctuation, abbreviations and more, *How to Use a Dictionary* resolves what most American curriculums never even bother to address: The moment one opens a dictionary,

*"What you want in education is to teach a person how to procure, absorb, use, evolve and relay knowledge. Those would be all the steps involved, and that is what should be done if one is trying to educate somebody."*

prepositions. Consequently, even common materials read for pleasure—paperback novels, for example—were not fully understood. Thus his conclusion that it was not for want of a so-called powerful vocabulary that one cannot effectively communicate; it was a failure to comprehend the building blocks upon which every larger vocabulary must rest.

What Mr. Hubbard's *Small Common Words Defined* offers, then, is a full understanding of those building blocks. In all, he defines the sixty most commonly used English words, once more utilizing illustrations for easy comprehension.

To then enable the student to build upon that vocabulary, he additionally offers his *How to Use a Dictionary*. Providing concise explanations of

even those for children, one immediately encounters terminology and derivation symbols that are neither generally understood nor adequately explained. Consequently, the student does not even possess *the* primary means for comprehending language; hence, Mr. Hubbard's solution for this problem as well.

What all these texts add up to, then, is a student who holds the veritable key to the English language—a firm grasp of how language is put together and how to most effectively use it for superior communication and better comprehension. Moreover, when taking into account the full body of Mr. Hubbard's educational breakthroughs, one is indeed looking at a revolution in learning. ■

# Applied Scholastics
# A Renaissance in Education

THROUGH THE EFFORTS OF APPLIED Scholastics International, a nonprofit public benefit corporation for the improvement of education globally, L. Ron Hubbard's Study Technology is presently at work in some seventy nations. It is also at work through entire curriculums and across whole school systems. Then, too, and all told, well over thirty million students have now participated in Applied Scholastics remedial projects across what previously represented the dead end of Western education.

To cite but a little of what ensues when Mr. Hubbard's technologies for learning and literacy come to the fore: a Los Angeles school district study revealed an average gain of 1.6 years in vocabulary and comprehension after only ten hours of tutoring in Study Technology; while not to put too fine an edge on it, one student actually gained over *five years* in test scores after only twenty hours of instruction. Instructors further reported an overall improvement in students' ability to learn, ability to read and a wholly unexpected improvement in classroom conduct.

An Arizona study tested students employing Study Technology after the commencement of a school year and again six months later. Results were similarly astonishing with standard reading tests revealing an average gain of two years in comprehension and vocabulary. Moreover, at four times expected gain, the achievement is especially remarkable for the fact no individual tutoring was provided.

In a South African class of underprivileged high-school students utilizing Mr. Hubbard's educational methods, gains were just as remarkable. At the end of a school year, students achieved no less than a 91 percent pass rate on Department of Education exams. Meanwhile, a control group, *sans* Study Technology, finished the year with a dismal 27 percent pass rate on the same said test.

In Mexico's Puebla State, habitually failing students were afforded a five-week course in Study Technology application. Immediately thereafter, test scores rose *three* times national averages and the Minister of Education implemented both a statewide Study Technology program and teacher-training academy within the Ministry itself.

In academically challenged schools of the Los Angeles inner-city community of Compton, Mr. Hubbard's Study Technology makes for equally transforming results: the equivalent achievement of two academic years

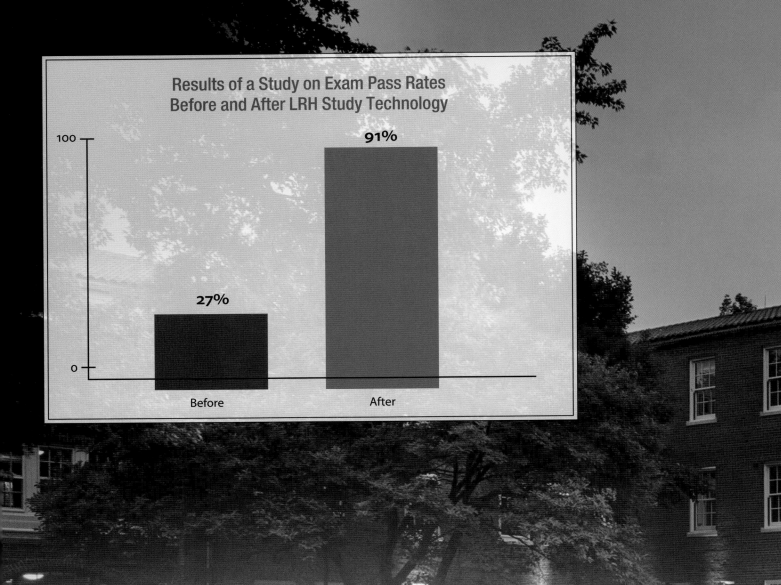

**Results of a Study on Exam Pass Rates Before and After LRH Study Technology**

100

91%

27%

0

Before          After

in but twenty to forty hours of part-time study, and this among recalcitrant and all but illiterate gang members.

The expressed aim, L. Ron Hubbard tells us, is to engender an expertise in the use and construction of language so that students may convey concepts and thoughts clearly and lucidly. Needless to say, and tragically so, the opposite is all too often the case, leaving whole generations without any real conception of the printed page or the intrinsic power of words.

But taking into account what Mr. Hubbard left us, there is indeed abundant hope; hence his summary point and an impassioned one at that: *let us enable young people to enjoy a lifetime of learning and a love of the written word.* ■

*For the complete body of information on Mr. Hubbard's solutions to education see the L. Ron Hubbard Series edition, Humanitarian: Education, Literacy & Civilization.*

The Applied Scholastics International Training Campus at Spanish Lake, Missouri:
Hub of a worldwide movement of and for Study Technology, it is here top
educators from every academic arena acquire Mr. Hubbard's tools for learning
and literacy. As those educators, in turn, train colleagues so it is that millions fulfill
L. Ron Hubbard's vision of reversing the "whole decay of Western education."

# Answers to
# Drugs

A LTHOUGH L. RON HUBBARD LONG RECOGNIZED WHAT drugs potentially spelled in terms of human misery, it was the so-called psychedelic revolution of the 1960s that prompted his most intensive work in the rehabilitation arena. His reasoning was simple—no one can be spiritually free if chained to a chemical substance.

Not only did drug abuse endanger one's health, but also one's learning rate, attitudes, personality and overall mental acuity. Indeed, following a 1973 review of what rampant drug use wrought among youths in New York City, he began to speak of this drug epidemic in terms of a devastating social cataclysm—and given what followed that psychedelic decade, including rampant cocaine and heroin consumption and all attendant violence therefrom, he was right. The social devastation proved very much a cataclysm. Nor was the problem in any way limited to street-drug consumption on the social fringe. On the contrary, with a psychiatric and pharmaceutical establishment intently pumping drugs into mainstream social arteries, the ramifications were altogether cultural. Moreover, with continued research through the late 1970s, yet another insidious

problem came to light: even years after quitting drugs and repairing all immediate damage, the former user remained at risk, and gravely so.

Central to the problem lay what Mr. Hubbard identified as tiny residues of previously ingested drugs lodged in fatty tissues. Liable to activate at any time, it is these residues that account for what is commonly termed the *flashback* and prove especially disturbing to those who experimented with LSD. Indeed, even years after ingestion, former drug users have found themselves on horrifying and unpredictable trips. Moreover, as Mr. Hubbard next discovered, street drugs were not the only detrimental substances to lodge in the fatty tissues. In fact, virtually every kind of drug, chemical poison, preservative, pesticide

The body of texts prescribing delivery of L. Ron Hubbard's Purification Program, including: *Clear Body, Clear Mind,* an illustrated workbook and technical materials to supervise the regimen

and industrial waste that we regularly ingest can likewise embed in the body and do us harm.

That discovery—and L. Ron Hubbard was unquestionably the first to recognize it—held profound ramifications. Consider, for example, a subsequent Environmental Protection Agency report admitting the average American consumes more than seven hundred potentially dangerous substances in the body. What all this spells in terms of ill health and shortened life, the agency cannot say. But one fact is patently clear from both Mr. Hubbard's original research and secondary medical studies: those toxic substances do much to diminish our ability to act, think and perceive.

The damage is done in this way: Given the body is essentially a communication system, with the brain acting as a switchboard for the translation of thought into action, biochemical substances can be devastating—actually disrupting the normal pattern of thought. Needless to say, these toxic substances also do much to inhibit our learning rate, our memory and all else necessary for our physical and spiritual well-being.

In answer to what he rightfully described as a biochemical crisis, Mr. Hubbard developed a complete program to counter it. It is most comprehensively explained in the book *Clear Body, Clear Mind* and utilizes an exact regimen of exercise, sauna and nutritional supplements under medical liaison. This, then, is the appropriately named *Purification Program* and intended to bring about detoxification,

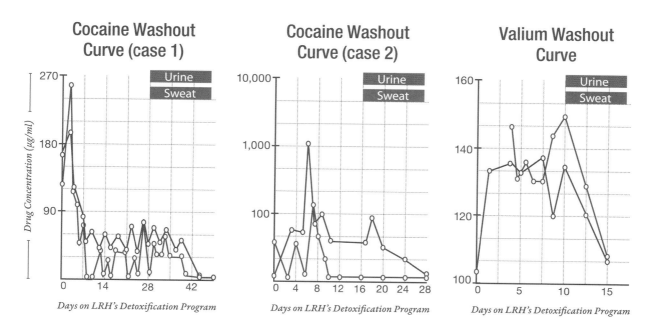

## Cocaine Washout Curve (case 1)

Drug Concentration (μg/ml)

Urine
Sweat

270
180
90

0    14    28    42

*Days on LRH's Detoxification Program*

## Cocaine Washout Curve (case 2)

Urine
Sweat

10,000
1,000
100

0  4  8  12  16  20  24  28

*Days on LRH's Detoxification Program*

## Valium Washout Curve

Urine
Sweat

160
140
120
100

0    5    10    15

*Days on LRH's Detoxification Program*

The Research Center for Dependency Disorders and Chronic Pain, in a recent scientific study of L. Ron Hubbard's Purification Program, found that residual drugs were definitely eliminated from the body, confirming Mr. Hubbard's findings.

*"As the developer of this sauna sweat-out program, L. Ron Hubbard found that drug residues/metabolites store in the fatty tissue of the body for long periods of time. I am amazed at the accuracy of his findings. The graphs and initial report show what we have expected for some time—drugs definitely are coming out during this program."*

*—Forest Tennant, M.D., Dr. P.H., Executive Director, Research Center for Dependency Disorders and Chronic Pain*

actually removing drug residuals from the fatty tissues.

To be sure, according to numerous studies, the Purification Program is the *only* means of ridding drug residues from fatty tissues. In point of fact, when Michigan residents were found to have ingested dangerous levels of a fire retardant in 1973, only the Purification Program proved capable of reducing toxin levels. Similarly, the program proved the only effective means for expunging airborne pollutants from 9/11 rescue personnel suffering pulmonary ailments; thus New York City firefighters describing the program as literally lifesaving.

The end result is more than impressive; it has factually redefined the parameters of environmental medicine. For whereas physicians previously treated only symptoms of toxic accumulation—including exhaustion, memory lapse and nausea—suddenly they were equipped to treat the underlying source of the problem. In consequence, many of those completing the program not only report improved perceptions, but also maintain they are generally happier, more energetic, mentally alert and altogether better disposed. Hence, the corollary reports of dramatically improved personal relationships and, in short, a recovery of what he so memorably described as:

*"...some of the happiness, some of the sincerity and some of the love and kindness with which he was created."* ■

Narconon New Life Program, Step One
**Learning How to LEARN**

Based on the works of
**L. RON HUBBARD**

The Basics of **COMMUNICATION**

Purification & **DETOXIFICATION**

Perception & **ORIENTATION**

Overcoming **UPS & DOWNS**

Personal Values & **INTEGRITY**

The Conditions of **EXISTENCE**

The Way to **HAPPINESS**

# *Narconon*
# Drug Rehabilitation

QUITE IN ADDITION TO L. RON Hubbard's Purification Program stands his larger rehabilitative regimen addressing not only what drugs spell in terms of mental and spiritual anguish, but also what led to usage in the first place; for unless *that* problem is resolved, one is forever left with the original condition for which drugs were a "solution." Also unique to Mr. Hubbard's rehabilitation program, and particularly relevant when considering the influence of opiates and crack cocaine, was his means of eliminating withdrawal pains. Traditionally resolved by simply substituting one addiction for another, e.g., methadone for heroin, the agony of withdrawal had long stood in the way of rehabilitating hard-core addicts. Not that much had ever been done on behalf of the die-hard addict; for unlike the recreational drug abuser, the long-term addict rarely possessed the wherewithal to pay for what passes for treatment in typical rehab clinics. In either case, however, with Mr. Hubbard's combination of nutritional supplements, therapeutic drills and exercises, the nightmare of hard-core withdrawal is no more.

To date, L. Ron Hubbard's drug rehabilitation methods are at work in some fifty nations and credited with salvaging tens of thousands of otherwise terminal addicts from drug dependence. Most notably, his methods are the mainstay of an international drug rehabilitation network known as *Narconon*. It is globally arrayed and internationally renowned for the fact Narconon consistently demonstrates at least three times the success rate of all other drug rehabilitation programs. Moreover, those successfully completing the program are not only drug-free, but also felony-free. If the point in any way seems obvious, it is not. Witness a seminal study revealing that 73 percent of those addicted to drugs also sold drugs. Following the completion of other rehabilitation programs, 37.9 percent continued dealing drugs. Among a similar group of addicts completing the Narconon program, not a single graduate trafficked in drugs. Likewise, whereas other programs were able to reduce drug-related robberies to 32.3 percent, those completing the Narconon program no longer committed any such crimes whatsoever.

It is no wonder, then, that the Narconon program is accredited by the prestigious Commission on Accreditation of Rehabilitation Facilities (CARF) as the benchmark for all rehabilitation programs. Exclusively based on L. Ron Hubbard's drug rehabilitation technology, the Narconon materials and program help thousands of hard-core addicts free themselves from the enslavement of drugs. ◼

*For the complete body of information on Mr. Hubbard's solutions to epidemic drug abuse see the L. Ron Hubbard Series edition, Humanitarian: Rehabilitating a Drugged Society.*

**Narconon Arrowhead on Lake Eufaula, Oklahoma: As hub of the international Narconon network, it is not only the world's largest residential treatment center, but also provides on-site training in L. Ron Hubbard's rehabilitation methods to rehab professionals from some twenty nations**

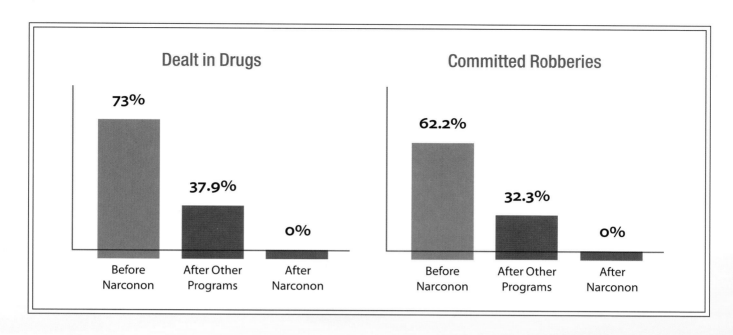

## Dealt in Drugs

73%
Before Narconon

37.9%
After Other Programs

0%
After Narconon

## Committed Robberies

62.2%
Before Narconon

32.3%
After Other Programs

0%
After Narconon

# The Way to

# HAPPINESS

A COMMON SENSE GUIDE TO BETTER LIVING

L. RON HUBBARD

THE WAY TO HAPPINESS FOUNDATION

# *The Way to* Happiness

EVERY CULTURE IN EVERY AGE HAS RELIED UPON A MORAL code to provide broad guidelines for conduct conducive to social accord and survival. Although much in past moral codes may not seem particularly relevant to this twenty-first century, when originally written they were entirely relevant. They helped ensure the perpetuation of the family, the group and nation. They provided the means by which people upheld the basic tenets of honesty and mutual trust. In short, the moral code supplied the overriding principles by which men could live peaceably, prosperously and in harmony with one another.

By the start of the 1980s, however, as L. Ron Hubbard so rightly observed, the world had become a veritable jungle. The signs were everywhere. "Greed is Good" went a popular aphorism of the day, while obscene fortunes were made through stock manipulation and fraud. If art and entertainment were any reflection, then the 1980s marked the beginning of a genuinely frightening era of casual and horrifically graphic violence. Then, too, who can forget what the 1980s signaled in terms of inner-city violence, where twelve- and thirteen-year-old children murdered one another with absolutely no compunction whatsoever; hence, the chilling resonance of such terms as "drive-by shooting" and "gangbang."

It was into this morally bereft landscape, then, that L. Ron Hubbard presented his *The Way to Happiness* in 1981. Typically, his approach was both historically and culturally broad. Just as all ancient cultures required a moral code to help sustain their fabric, he declared, so too did our own; for old values had been broken yet not replaced by new, while religiously based codes of ages past demanded a faith many could no longer muster. Nor, he concluded, were theories that children would naturally assume a moral stance any more reliable. Thus he wrote *The Way to Happiness*.

The work stands alone as the only moral code aimed at a pragmatic, high-tech and highly cynical society. The first work of its kind based wholly on common sense, it is entirely embracive. It carries no other appeal than to the good sense of readers and is designed to help them actually apply its precepts in their daily lives. Beneath the many differences of national, political, racial, religious or other hue, each of us as individuals must make our way through life. Such a way, *The Way to Happiness* teaches, can be made better if the precepts it presents are known and followed.

Life in an immoral society can be more than simply difficult when basic human values are held up to ridicule. To counter such declining moral trends, Mr. Hubbard's *The Way to Happiness* contains 21 separate precepts—each constituting a rule for living relevant to anyone in our global village. Indeed, more than one hundred million copies of the booklet in better than two hundred nations and a hundred languages are presently in circulation, with no end in sight. The work has further inspired scores of United States Congressional recognitions and many more heartfelt endorsements by police, civic leaders, businessmen and educators. It forms the basis of the highly successful "Set a Good Example" and "Get Drugs Off School Grounds" campaigns, involving over twelve million American students, parents and teachers in upwards of twelve thousand

The three editions of L. Ron Hubbard's *The Way to Happiness:* hardback, booklet and a book on film

elementary, junior high and high schools. These campaigns, in turn, additionally earned endorsements from some 90 state governors and state legislators, as well as directors of drug abuse programs and departments of education in hundreds of American communities.

The praise is well deserved. One Ohio school, prior to participation in a *Way to Happiness* program, suffered both routine violence and drug abuse while students tested well below acceptable reading levels. After a two-year *Way to Happiness* drive, those trends dramatically reversed and the school was declared entirely drug-free while reading levels soared well above national averages.

> *"Happiness lies in engaging in worthwhile activities. But there is only one person who for certain can tell what will make one happy—oneself."*

In a notoriously violent South Central Los Angeles results from *The Way to Happiness* distribution were likewise nothing short of miraculous. Indeed, after hard-core gang members read (or were read to) *The Way to Happiness,* they voluntarily removed graffiti from 130 neighborhood buildings, while voluntarily passing out hundreds of copies of the booklet to local residents. The booklet

# Moral Precepts from The Way to Happiness

1. TAKE CARE OF YOURSELF.

2. BE TEMPERATE.

3. DON'T BE PROMISCUOUS.

4. LOVE AND HELP CHILDREN.

5. HONOR AND HELP YOUR PARENTS.

6. SET A GOOD EXAMPLE.

7. SEEK TO LIVE WITH THE TRUTH.

8. DO NOT MURDER.

9. DON'T DO ANYTHING ILLEGAL.

10. SUPPORT A GOVERNMENT DESIGNED AND RUN FOR ALL THE PEOPLE.

11. DO NOT HARM A PERSON OF GOOD WILL.

12. SAFEGUARD AND IMPROVE YOUR ENVIRONMENT.

13. DO NOT STEAL.

14. BE WORTHY OF TRUST.

15. FULFILL YOUR OBLIGATIONS.

16. BE INDUSTRIOUS.

17. BE COMPETENT.

18. RESPECT THE RELIGIOUS BELIEFS OF OTHERS.

19. TRY NOT TO DO THINGS TO OTHERS THAT YOU WOULD NOT LIKE THEM TO DO TO YOU.

20. TRY TO TREAT OTHERS AS YOU WOULD WANT THEM TO TREAT YOU.

21. FLOURISH AND PROSPER.

Titles of the 21 precepts: With the full body of text accompanying these precepts, readers are presented with nothing less than a comprehensive guide to living and thus what indeed comprises a Way to Happiness

Aceh

Afrikaans

Albanian

Amharic

Arabic

Armenian

Burmese

Catalan

Cebuano

Chavacano

Chinese

Chinese Traditional

English

Ewe

Farsi

Filipino

Finnish

French

Hausa

Hebrew

Hiligaynon

Hindi

Hungarian

Icelandic

Italian

Japanese

Jawa Kromo

Kannada

Kapampangan

Kazakh

Lakskiy

Latvian

Lithuanian

Macedonian

Malagasy

Malay

Norwegian

Pangasinan

Pashto

Polish

Portuguese

Portuguese Brazilian

Siswati

Slovak

Slovenian

Somali

Spanish Castilian

Spanish Latin American

Tigrigna

Tigrinya

Turkish

Turkmen

Ukranian

Urdu

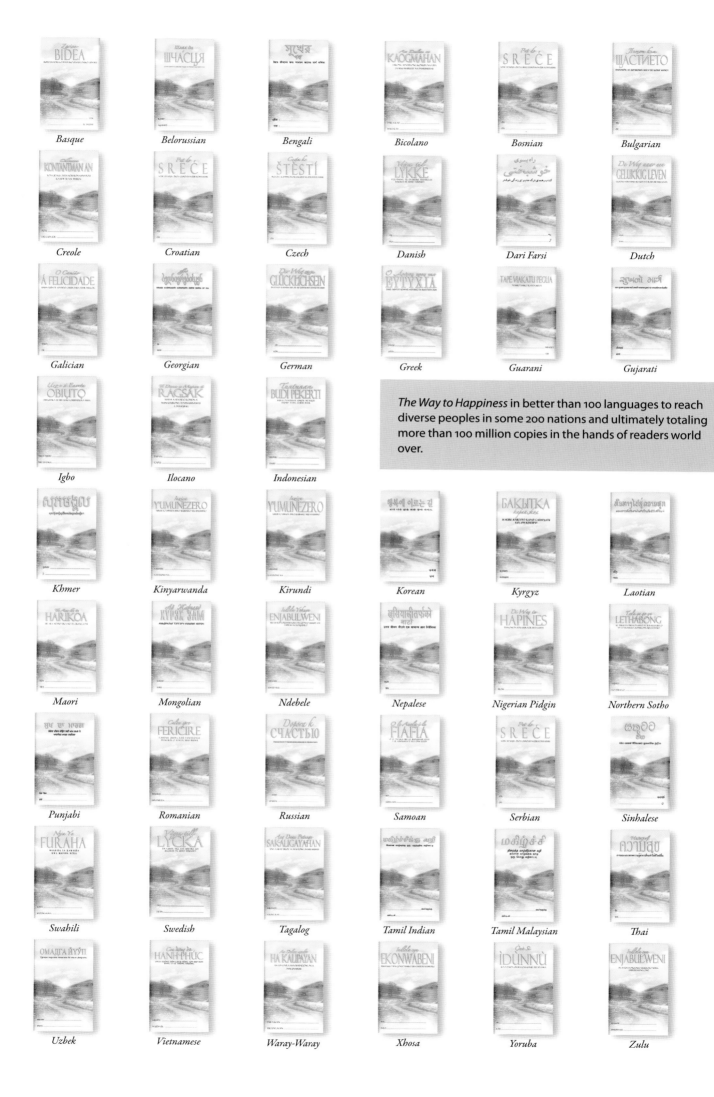

Basque

Belorussian

Bengali

Bicolano

Bosnian

Bulgarian

Creole

Croatian

Czech

Danish

Dari Farsi

Dutch

Galician

Georgian

German

Greek

Guarani

Gujarati

Igbo

Ilocano

Indonesian

*The Way to Happiness* in better than 100 languages to reach diverse peoples in some 200 nations and ultimately totaling more than 100 million copies in the hands of readers world over.

Khmer

Kinyarwanda

Kirundi

Korean

Kyrgyz

Laotian

Maori

Mongolian

Ndebele

Nepalese

Nigerian Pidgin

Northern Sotho

Punjabi

Romanian

Russian

Samoan

Serbian

Sinhalese

Swahili

Swedish

Tagalog

Tamil Indian

Tamil Malaysian

Thai

Uzbek

Vietnamese

Waray-Waray

Xhosa

Yoruba

Zulu

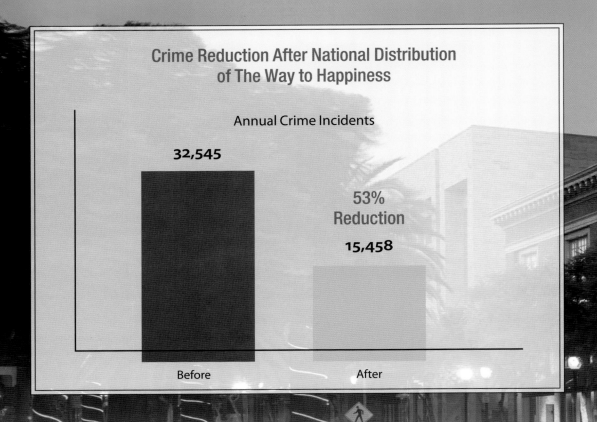

**Crime Reduction After National Distribution
of The Way to Happiness**

Annual Crime Incidents

32,545

53%
Reduction

15,458

Before         After

also inspired food drives and cleanup efforts in the wake of the 1992 Los Angeles riots and the same again in the 1994 Los Angeles earthquake. As a community leader from the Parents of Watts group reported: "We've been giving out this book now for about two or three months. Nothing different has come into the community except this particular book—and we do see a change and we have to relate it to *The Way to Happiness*."

Internationally, Mr. Hubbard's *The Way to Happiness* similarly proves a significant catalyst for positive change. In the South African township of Soweto, for example, a campaign based on the precept "Safeguard and Improve Your Environment" garnered support from the largest national food chain and labor unions, after booklet distribution dramatically improved community relations. As one resident

explained: "The rate of violence has decreased so much that we now know how to sit down together and share our views. This relationship comes from your wonderful booklets." Still another campaign in the South African city of Pietermaritzburg proved so successful in easing racial tensions, the South African police requested 114,000 copies of *The Way to Happiness* booklet—one for every officer in the nation. Likewise adopting the booklet in whole cloth are Anglican and Pentecostal Churches across South Africa's Gauteng Province and the same again across the Eastern Cape.

There is substantially more. Moscow law enforcement officers carry copies of *The Way to Happiness* prefaced with a statement reading: "This book is recommended to you by the Moscow City Police Department in the hopes that it will help you lead a better and happier

life." The booklet was additionally reprinted in the city's largest newspaper for the fact it has repeatedly proven a calming influence among restive populations. To cite but two examples: a national proliferation of booklets is now on record for quelling political violence in Thailand, while *The Way to Happiness* seeded through Congolese rebel factions led to an actual laying down of arms.

For all the above reasons and more, *The Way to Happiness* comprises a movement unto itself in Colombia. Declaring the root of Colombian violence lay "not in politics, but in the soul of our people," publishers of *El Tiempo* reprinted selections of the booklet to calm general unrest. To the same end, Colombian military commanders ordered thirty thousand copies of the booklet distributed to soldiers on narcopolitical firing lines even as a National Coordinator for the

Juvenile Police directed distribution through some forty patrol units. Not to be outdone, the Minister of Education further sanctioned the booklet as a supplementary teaching aid for all elementary curriculums. Thereafter, and absolutely date coincident, drug-related murder plummeted to the lowest point in decades.

Today, of course, the popular assault on moral decline is pervasive. It is addressed by virtually every political referendum and inspires any number of articles, books and documentaries. To what degree this shrill cry for a moral resurgence has, in turn, been inspired by Mr. Hubbard's work is, of course, difficult to say. But with *The Way to Happiness,* he has clearly charted a course toward greater tolerance, peace and mutual trust. ■

The Way to Happiness Foundation International in Glendale, California, where global distribution is coordinated across more than two hundred nations to better than one hundred million people

Improving **Conditions**

Improving Conditions

How to Deal with Ups & Do

Confronting & Comm

The Fundame

# *Criminon*
# Restoring Honor and Self-Respect

No discussion of *The Way to Happiness* would be complete without a word regarding the criminal-reform program utilizing that booklet. Known as *Criminon* (without crime), this program is derived from Mr. Hubbard's discoveries on causes and prevention of crime as determined through the course of research conducted while serving as a Los Angeles law enforcement officer in the late 1940s. "If you want to rehabilitate a criminal," he declared, "just go back and find out when he *did* lose his personal pride. Rehabilitate that one point and you don't have a criminal anymore." With Mr. Hubbard's *The Way to Happiness* and key principles drawn from Scientology fundamentals, Criminon accomplishes exactly that.

Again, the program is unique. As with Narconon, it relies upon no drugs or punishment, but rather appeals to what Mr. Hubbard described as the basic goodness within all men. If such an approach seems unlikely among hardened criminals, the results speak for themselves. Headquartered in Los Angeles, Criminon delivers through correspondence courses and directly on the floor of penitentiary cellblocks. It further delivers in every *type* of facility: maximum security, medium security, minimum security, county jails and juvenile halls.

In one such juvenile program alone, wherein 80 percent of all young offenders were routinely rearrested, a Criminon regimen utterly reversed the trend. That is, 90 percent of those completing The Way to Happiness Course were *not* rearrested. It is not for nothing, then, Chief Probation Officer, Daniel O. Black of the Butler County Juvenile Court in Greenville, Alabama, concluded: "The Juvenile Justice System is in great need of a workable community-based first-step program. *The Way to Happiness* fills that void. We start with basics: a good moral foundation based on honesty, integrity and trust; that is *The Way to Happiness*."

There is appreciably more and it is equally impressive. No words can adequately express what it means to witness the "transformation of a criminal into a human being," writes a correctional officer in the wake of Criminon implementation across Mexican penitentiaries. Nor is the statement in any way isolated. To be sure, Criminon now delivers in more than 1,500 penal institutions across some fifty nations and results are similarly regarded with awe.

To cite but the merest fraction of it: a notorious

Leeuwkop supermax penitentiary in South Africa saw a 90 percent recidivism rate plummet to barely 2 percent after implementation of Criminon. Moreover, pervasive cellblock violence fell to virtually nothing. The numbers are no less telling across Indonesian facilities—habitually high recidivism likewise dropping to 2 percent—whereupon Indonesia recommends Criminon implementation to all neighboring nations. Then there's Rwanda, where a 60 percent recidivism rate fell to zero and where wardens frequently mistake Criminon graduates for correctional officers "because of the type of behavior they conform to."

All told, better than one hundred thousand inmates have successfully participated in Criminon programs and since embarked on crime-free lives. What those former inmates represent in totality is no less than the total sum and substance of what L. Ron Hubbard long maintained—namely and most sincerely: for all Man's failings, his violence and degradation, the human being is nonetheless basically good and so, as he further tells us:

*"Wherever Man strives, wherever he works, whatever he does, the good he does outweighs the evil."* ∎

*For the complete body of information on The Way to Happiness see the L. Ron Hubbard Series edition, Humanitarian: Restoring Honor & Self-Respect.*

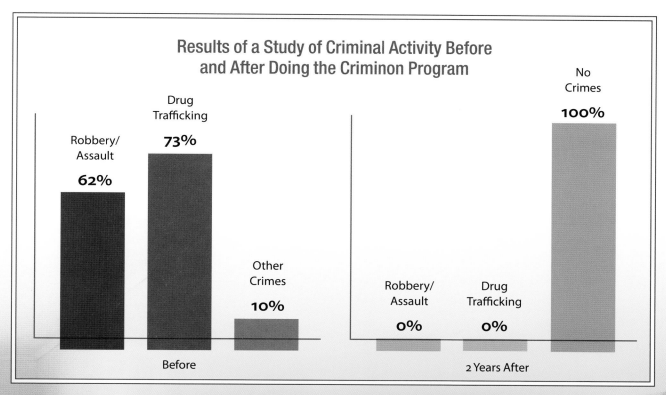

## Results of a Study of Criminal Activity Before and After Doing the Criminon Program

**Before**

Robbery/Assault **62%**

Drug Trafficking **73%**

Other Crimes **10%**

**2 Years After**

Robbery/Assault **0%**

Drug Trafficking **0%**

No Crimes **100%**

Organization Executive Course

Organization Executive Course

L. Ron Hubbard

L. Ron Hubbard

Basic Staff Hat
0

HCO Division
1

2

3

## Solutions to
# Administration

"IT IS NOT MAN'S DREAMS THAT FAIL HIM," DECLARED L. RON Hubbard. "It is the lack of know-how required to bring those dreams into actuality." For that reason and that reason alone, "Whole nations, to say nothing of commercial firms or societies or groups, have spent decades in floundering turmoil."

The consequences stare back at us as headlines every day: crippling deficits, onerous taxation, failing businesses and, even in an ostensibly prosperous United States, some forty million people live below the poverty line. It is not for nothing, then, that Mr. Hubbard further declared: "Man's happiness and the longevity of companies and states apparently depend upon organizational know-how."

If one genuinely understood how individuals best function—their needs, aspirations and the source of their failings—one would naturally understand how groups of individuals best function. Such was the stance from which L. Ron Hubbard addressed the problems of how we cooperate with others—not with administrative gimmicks or authoritarian decrees, but with a uniquely compassionate view of groups as individuals united in a common purpose.

In all, Mr. Hubbard spent more than three decades developing and codifying the administrative policies by which Scientology organizations function. These policies are derived from the fundamental laws governing all human behavior and thus constitute a body of knowledge as important to the subject of groups as his writings on Dianetics and Scientology are to the rehabilitation of the human spirit. Indeed, until Dianetics and Scientology, no one actually knew principles governing group activities any more than they knew principles governing the human mind.

At the heart of Mr. Hubbard's administrative discoveries is the Organizing Board, or "Org Board" as it is more generally known. Developed in 1965, the Org Board is the diagrammatic pattern of organization, delineating every function relative to successful group activity.

## EXECUTIVE DIVISION
### DIVISION 7

## COMMUNICATIONS DIVISION
### DIVISION 1

## DISSEMINATION DIVISION
### DIVISION 2

The Organizing Board developed by L. Ron Hubbard contains seven divisions, each with specific duties and functions. All of Mr. Hubbard's administrative technology is contained in the eight volume *Organization Executive Course. Volume 0* (below), the *Basic Staff Hat,* contains all policies pertinent to any staff member of an organization. The seven remaining volumes, numbered 1 through 7, correspond to the same numbered divisions of the Organizing Board. Each divisional volume contains all the policies pertaining to the purpose and functions of that division.

The Executive Division coordinates and supervises the organization's activities so it runs smoothly, produces its products viably and delivers its products and services to individuals and the community in high quality. It successfully runs the activity through the following functions:

• Does the organization's planning and gets it executed so objectives are achieved.

• Sees to it that the technology and policy of the organization is followed without deviation.

• Ensures that the organization's premises are in good repair and acquires additional space to accommodate expansion.

• Maintains proper governmental relations and cares for legal affairs.

• In the case of a company, this division could include the office of the person who started the organization or the one who had developed the product produced by the company.

The Communications Division is fully responsible for the establishment of the organization. It accomplishes this through the following actions:

• Hires eligible staff and properly places them for the benefit of the individual and the organization.

• Sees that new and existing staff know how to do their jobs.

• Sets up standard communications systems and gets in established communication routes so that all communications to and from the public and internally in the organization are swiftly and properly handled.

• Collects and accurately graphs the organization's statistics for executive use.

• Maintains a high level of ethical behavior among the staff.

• Inspects the organization's activities so any difficulties inhibiting expansion are detected and reported upon to the proper executive for swift resolution.

The Dissemination Division makes the organization's products and services widely known and demanded, creating a high volume of public attaining them. To achieve this, the following actions are done:

• Uses informative mailings, magazines, promotion and other communication methods to inform the public of the organization's services and products and the published materials it offers so these are acquired in a viable quantity.

• Stocks all published materials so they are readily available.

• Contacts individuals who have expressed interest in the organization's products so these are obtained by them.

• Keeps accurate files of people who previously received service or obtained products from the organization and maintains correspondence with them so they can acquire further products and services.

**EXECUTIVE DIRECTOR**

**ORGANIZATION EXECUTIVE SECRETARY**

## TREASURY DIVISION
### DIVISION 3

The Treasury Division handles the financial matters of the organization so its physical body is fully cared for, enabling it to produce its products and deliver its services and remain solvent. Its functions include the following:

- Handles incoming funds received in exchange for the organization's products so these are properly recorded.
- Disburses funds for purchasing and the payment of all bills, as well as pays the staff, so its financial obligations are fulfilled and the other divisions have the wherewithal to produce their products.
- Keeps precise records of all financial transactions, does any necessary bookkeeping and financial reports, and preserves all assets and reserves.

## PRODUCTION DIVISION
### DIVISION 4

The Production Division is where the actual products of the organization are produced. It achieves its purposes by performing the following actions:

- Ensures that the wherewithal and resources for production are made available.
- Schedules production for maximum efficiency and service to the public.
- Produces the organization's product and delivers its services rapidly in high quantity and with excellent quality so people are satisfied with results.

## QUALIFICATIONS DIVISION
### DIVISION 5

The Qualifications Division sees that every product leaving the organization has attained the expected level of quality. To accomplish this it does the following:

- Examines the validity and correctness of products and passes these to review or certification so every product is certified, or corrected so it can be certified as achieving the organization's standard of product quality.
- Reviews the organization's product to isolate the causes for any lower-than-acceptable level of quality.
- Reviews staff actions and corrects them where needed so technology and policy are applied with superb results.
- Cares for the staff as individuals so they become fully trained in all aspects of their jobs and organizational policy and technology and become competent, contributing group members.

## PUBLIC DIVISION
### DIVISION 6

The Public Division, through all of its activities, brings knowledge of and distributes the organization's services and products to the broad public. To accomplish this, it sees that the following activities occur:

- Ensures that the appearance of the organization and its personnel are excellent.
- Makes the organization and its services and products well known to the community.
- Works with community groups and other organizations to improve society.
- Establishes and makes productive distribution points outside the organization which offer its services and products to new public.
- Records and makes widely known the success of the organization's activities and its products.

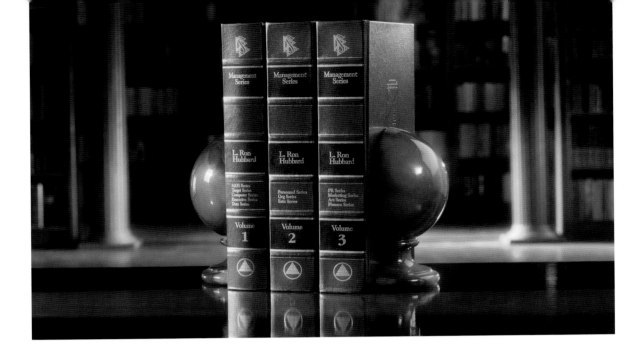

L. Ron Hubbard's *Management Series* Volumes contain all tools needed for successful, high-level management including breakthrough administrative technology concerning personnel, organizing and management

In fact, the Org Board actually describes the ideal organizational pattern for *any* activity.

That pattern delineates activities—be it group *or* individual—in terms of seven essential divisions. Those divisions, in turn, lay out all duties, positions and functions necessary for a coordinated effort. The divisions 1 through 7 of the Organizing Board are laid out in a sequence known as the *Cycle of Production*. Again, this sequence is in no way based upon an arbitrary. When Mr. Hubbard speaks of a production cycle, he is not speaking in terms of an assembly line or the human machine that constitutes the organizational pattern in the corporate world. Rather, he is speaking of those specific activities that all production, whether individual or group, naturally follows. In point of fact: if one wishes to accomplish *anything,* he must perform these seven basic steps. In that respect, the Organizing Board is not simply the ideal method of successful organization; it is actually the *only* method of successful organization.

Having defined the ideal organizational form, Mr. Hubbard next provides the specific administrative policies upon which that form functions. These administrative policies are contained in a set of reference texts known as the *Organization Executive Course* (OEC).

The *OEC Volumes* provide the theory and particulars of every working facet in an organization—from hiring personnel to the ethical conduct of employees, from promotion to quality control and more. In fact, there is a volume corresponding to each division of the Org Board, describing the exact operations and functions of that division.

In additional volumes known as *The Management Series,* Mr. Hubbard provides all an executive need know on the subject of how to manage an organization. Included therein: how to organize, how to function as an executive, how to establish, how to handle personnel and even the art of public relations. Thus, the *OEC Volumes* provide the policies by which one runs an organization, while *The Management Series* provides the policies by which organizations are managed.

Among the principles found in these policies is the very key *Conditions of Existence,* which Mr. Hubbard defined in terms of the degrees of success or survival. The basic concept is vaguely known to the astute administrator who speaks in terms of "corporate health." But whereas the idea of corporate health implies only two states—good or bad—and offers no precise means of improving that health,

L. Ron Hubbard provides a great deal more. Specifically, Mr. Hubbard analyzed the various degrees of survival—from a non-existence state to a dangerous situation, to a condition

or individual. Administratively, then, the statistic provides the barometer of organizational health, while Mr. Hubbard's Condition Formulas provide the means for improving that state of

*"To be effective and successful a manager must understand as fully as possible the goals and aims of the group he manages.... He must be able to tolerate and better the practical attainments and advances of which his group and its members may be capable. He must strive to narrow, always, the ever-existing gulf between the ideal and the practical."*

of emergency to one of normal, affluence and power. Moreover, he has spelled out the necessary *Condition Formulas,* or actions, one must take for the improvement of any condition. That is, by simply performing the outlined steps, one rises through each condition to the next until one's organization is indeed thriving.

To eliminate any guesswork as to one's operating condition, Mr. Hubbard further delineates methods of monitoring organizational health by statistics. The statistic, as he defines it, is a number or amount compared to an earlier number or amount of the same thing. Thus, statistics refer to the quantity of work done or the value of it and are the only sound measure of any production or any activity, be it organizational

health. Correctly utilized, these tools allow for precise isolation of troublesome areas and how to improve those trouble spots.

Given what Mr. Hubbard's administrative breakthroughs represent in terms of providing rules by which groups ideally function, it was inevitable that his administrative discoveries would become much in demand throughout general industry and elsewhere. Accordingly, and expressly to meet that demand, the Hubbard Colleges of Administration were founded.

These institutions specifically utilize L. Ron Hubbard's works for the enhancement of a professional's ability to tackle the challenges of administering and running a group, company

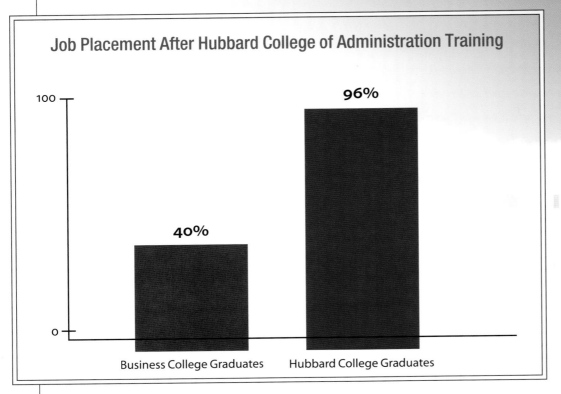

## Job Placement After Hubbard College of Administration Training

100

96%

40%

0

Business College Graduates    Hubbard College Graduates

The Hubbard College of Administration International in Los Angeles, California: The academic seat of the worldwide Hubbard College network, the Los Angeles campus welcomes students from some 25 countries and is the only institution of its kind boasting a 96 percent job placement for program graduates

or organization. Headquartered in Los Angeles, the network now extends across five continents. It provides training in L. Ron Hubbard's administrative methods to businessmen and women from all arenas: heavy industry, service industry, entertainment, communications, healthcare and every imaginable professional service. As the international flagship, the degree-granting Los Angeles institution further sees enrollments from well over a dozen nations and particularly Asia, where innovative managerial methods are especially in demand.

Also of note is the use of L. Ron Hubbard's administrative methods in former communist countries where the privatization of industry necessitated an entirely new organizational philosophy. Russia, for example, boasts a Hubbard College of Administration in Moscow and it has seeded L. Ron Hubbard administrative tools across the whole economic infrastructure. Through the same privatization process, Hungarian administrators likewise turned to L. Ron Hubbard's organizational policies and so established a Hubbard College in Budapest. Albeit in a very different economic

climate, a substantial number of Colombia's federal employees similarly boast Hubbard College training, as do state and county employees of Texas.

Recession, inflation, sagging productivity, debts, strikes, unemployment, poverty and want—these all-too-familiar symptoms of economic decline are actually indicators of a much deeper problem: a crippling lack of administrative know-how. If today's businesses and governments could competently apply the basic principles of organization and administration, they would enact workable solutions to what has become economic chaos. Such is the role of L. Ron Hubbard's administrative technology: to provide the means whereby businesses might prosper, governments rule wisely, people may be free of economic duress and, in short, failed dreams may be revived. ∎

**Multiple exposure, 1965;
photograph by L. Ron Hubbard**

# PART THREE

# ARTIST

# Artist

"FOR SOME FIFTEEN YEARS," DECLARED L. RON HUBBARD IN A pivotal essay from 1965, "I have been studying, among other branches of philosophy, the subject of ART."

His reasons were twofold. First and foremost, as he explained, "Art is the least-codified of human endeavors and the most misunderstood." Even its very definition, he noted, was still subject to intense debate. Thus, on a purely academic level, he wished to examine the subject in its broadest and most essential terms, and thereby resolve questions philosophers and critics have long pondered, including that most basic of all questions, *"What is Art?"*

Yet there was another reason for his interest in the subject and it follows from the fact that quite apart from all else L. Ron Hubbard accomplished, he was himself an artist. Hence this from thirty years preceding:

*"Capturing my own dreams in words, paint or music and then seeing them live is the highest kind of excitement."*

While later and as an all-encompassing statement from the cusp of Scientology:

*"The artist has an enormous role in the enhancement of today's and the creation of tomorrow's reality. He operates in a rank in advance of science as to the necessities and requirements of Man. The elevation of a culture can be measured directly by the numbers of its people working in the field of aesthetics. Because the artist deals in future realities, he always seeks improvements or changes in the existing reality. This makes the artist, inevitably and invariably, a rebel against the status quo. The artist, day by day, by postulating the new realities of the future, accomplishes peaceful revolution."*

Unquestionably, then, "This rather vast subject of ART," as he described it, was not one he took lightly and, in fact, it is probably impossible to consider the life of L. Ron Hubbard without considering his artistic achievements. ■

# Writer

"WHAT IS GENERALLY MISSED," L. RON HUBBARD ONCE remarked, "is that my writing financed research." Nevertheless and notwithstanding all that ensued from his research, L. Ron Hubbard's literary legacy is of a stature unto itself. Having published a full fifteen million words between 1929 and 1941,

the name L. Ron Hubbard was virtually synonymous with popular fiction through the 1930s and '40s. In point of fact, as friend and fellow author Frederik Pohl proclaimed: "The instant Ron's stories appeared on the newsstands, they were part of every fan's cultural heritage." And given the volume of Mr. Hubbard's output through these years—more than two hundred stories and novels spanning all popular genres, including mystery, western, adventure, fantasy, science fiction and even romance—that cultural heritage was indeed rich.

Appropriately, Mr. Hubbard's primary outlet through these years was the pulps. Named for the pulpwood stock on which they were printed, the pulps were easily the most popular literary publication of their day. In fact, with some 30 million regular readers—a quarter of the American population—their impact was quite unrivaled until the advent of television. But if the pulps were first and foremost a popular vehicle, they were by no means without literary merit. Among others to launch their careers in the likes of *Argosy, Astounding Science Fiction, Black Mask* and *Five-Novels Monthly* were Raymond Chandler, Dashiell Hammett, Edgar Rice Burroughs and Robert Heinlein. It was not for nothing, then, that Mr. Hubbard would fondly look back on these "dear old days" to tell of evenings spent with the great Dash Hammett, Edgar "Tarzan" Burroughs and Mr. Pulps himself, Arthur J. Burks. But if Mr. Hubbard would not particularly speak of his own status, it was no less legendary.

The fabulous world of the pulps where L. Ron Hubbard reigned supreme for nearly two decades: As even a cursory glance at magazines presenting his work suggests, his tales spanned every conceivable genre—from intergalactic travel to westerns, mysteries, adventure and even romance.

> *"In writing an adventure story a writer has to know that he is adventuring for a lot of people who cannot. The writer has to take them here and there about the globe and show them excitement and love and realism."*
>
> —L. Ron Hubbard

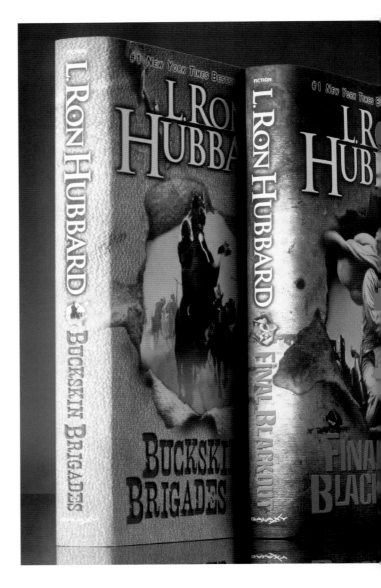

As a matter of fact, recalled Pohl, "Nobody was doing the sort of thing he did any better...colorful, exciting, continually challenging." The case in point is L. Ron Hubbard's full-length novel, *Buckskin Brigades.* Acclaimed as the first work to offer an accurate portrait of the Blackfeet Indians, *Buckskin Brigades* was all that Pohl described and more. A "decidedly rare type of romance," declared the *New York Times,* and pointed to the fact it presented the first real reversal of what comprised a fairly ethnocentric cliché, i.e., the Native American as a murderous savage. Indeed, as Council Members of the Blackfeet Nation were to later declare, "Never have our morals and ethics been presented with such clarity." Additionally marking *Buckskin Brigades* as unique is the fact it once again rose to the bestseller lists some fifty years after original publication.

Also generally remarked upon in reference to L. Ron Hubbard's work through the 1930s was his truly astonishing versatility and rate of production. If one needed a story on a Monday, explained Standard Magazines' Editor Jack Schiff, one only had to telephone Ron Hubbard on a Friday—and the statement was no exaggeration. With a regular production of some 70,000 to 100,000 words a month, Mr. Hubbard became a king of high-speed

production writers (and that at only three days a week and in every imaginable genre).

As a Hollywood screenwriter during this same era, his high-volume production on such films as Columbia's *The Mysterious Pilot* and *The Great Adventures of Wild Bill Hickok* and Warner Brothers' *The Spider Returns* is likewise still remembered; and all the more so, inasmuch as L. Ron Hubbard's *The Secret of Treasure Island* stands among the most profitable serials of the era. Nor was Mr. Hubbard's 1937 stint in Hollywood his only contribution to the medium; for, in fact, among his last works through the 1970s and '80s are several screenplays in a variety of genres.

Yet however varied and prodigious his output, no discussion of L. Ron Hubbard's

role in American fiction is complete without considering his hand in reshaping science fiction and his truly indelible stamp on fantasy.

The year was 1938, and if L. Ron Hubbard was not yet exactly a household name, his byline on the cover of a *Thrilling Adventures* or *Five-Novels Monthly* was guaranteed to instantly boost circulation. (The same was also true for a number of L. Ron Hubbard pseudonyms employed to span the various genres.) Hoping to capitalize on precisely that popularity, publishing giant Street & Smith enlisted Mr. Hubbard to imbue their newly acquired *Astounding Science Fiction* with a touch of literary excellence. Although not particularly familiar with the genre, Mr. Hubbard was nonetheless intrigued

with the proposal. Whereas *Astounding* had previously focused on improbable machinery—spaceships, ray guns and robots—Street & Smith decreed the magazine must take a more human turn with fully realized characters, i.e., *"real people."*

The result was a body of fiction to forever live in the canon of speculative fiction. To cite but one seminal classic, there was L. Ron Hubbard's *Final Blackout,* which Robert Heinlein declared to be "as perfect a piece of science fiction as has ever been written." Also from this arrangement with Street & Smith came L. Ron Hubbard's foray into the fantasy genre and his landmark work of the era, *Fear.* Drawn from his ethnological research, *Fear* tells of a clash between science and superstition that eventually led horror master Stephen King to call it "One of the few books in the chiller genre which actually merits employment of the overworked adjective 'classic,' as in 'This is a classic tale of creeping, surreal menace and horror.'"

*Fear,* however, was by no means the only L. Ron Hubbard work to merit that classic adjective. After a thirty-year absence from fiction to devote himself to the development of Dianetics and Scientology, and in celebration of his 50th year as a professional writer, Mr. Hubbard returned in the 1980s with two monumental works: *Battlefield Earth,* science fiction's largest single-volume epic and the ten-volume, 1.2 million word *Mission Earth.*

Heralded as a "huge, rollicking saga," with what A. E. van Vogt called "the great pulp music in every line," *Battlefield Earth* is a novel of legendary proportions and still remains among the bestselling titles in science fiction history. Moreover, it was the first bestseller of the genre in more than a decade and continued riding the lists for a phenomenal eight months after original publication. As such, it was rightly credited with returning science fiction to the forefront of popular literature and otherwise stands as an unqualified landmark. Accordingly, it earned the Academy of Science Fiction, Fantasy and Horror Films' *Golden Scroll Award* as well as the Academy's *Saturn Award.* The work was additionally honored with Italy's *Tetradramma*

*d'Oro Award* (for the story's inherent message of peace) and a special *Gutenberg Award* as an exceptional contribution to the genre.

No less acclaimed was the ten-volume *Mission Earth* series earning the *Cosmos 2000 Award* from French readers and the *Nova Science Fiction Award* from Italy's National Committee for Science Fiction and Fantasy (a particular honor inasmuch as Mr. Hubbard was the first non-Italian to receive the award). The series is also remembered for the fact each and every volume immediately rose to international bestseller lists—an unmatched feat in publishing history.

But even so, the later novels of L. Ron Hubbard continued making history. *Battlefield*

*Earth,* for example, repeatedly returned to bestseller lists and was latterly voted among the top three hundred best English-language novels of the last hundred years. Moreover, along with his works of nonfiction, no less than thirty L. Ron Hubbard titles consecutively appeared on international bestseller lists in the 1980s and 1990s—yet another feat unmatched in the annals of publishing history. Both *Mission Earth* and *Battlefield Earth* further stand as model works for creative writing in numerous colleges and universities; while L. Ron Hubbard himself now stands among the most widely read authors of this or any other age. ∎

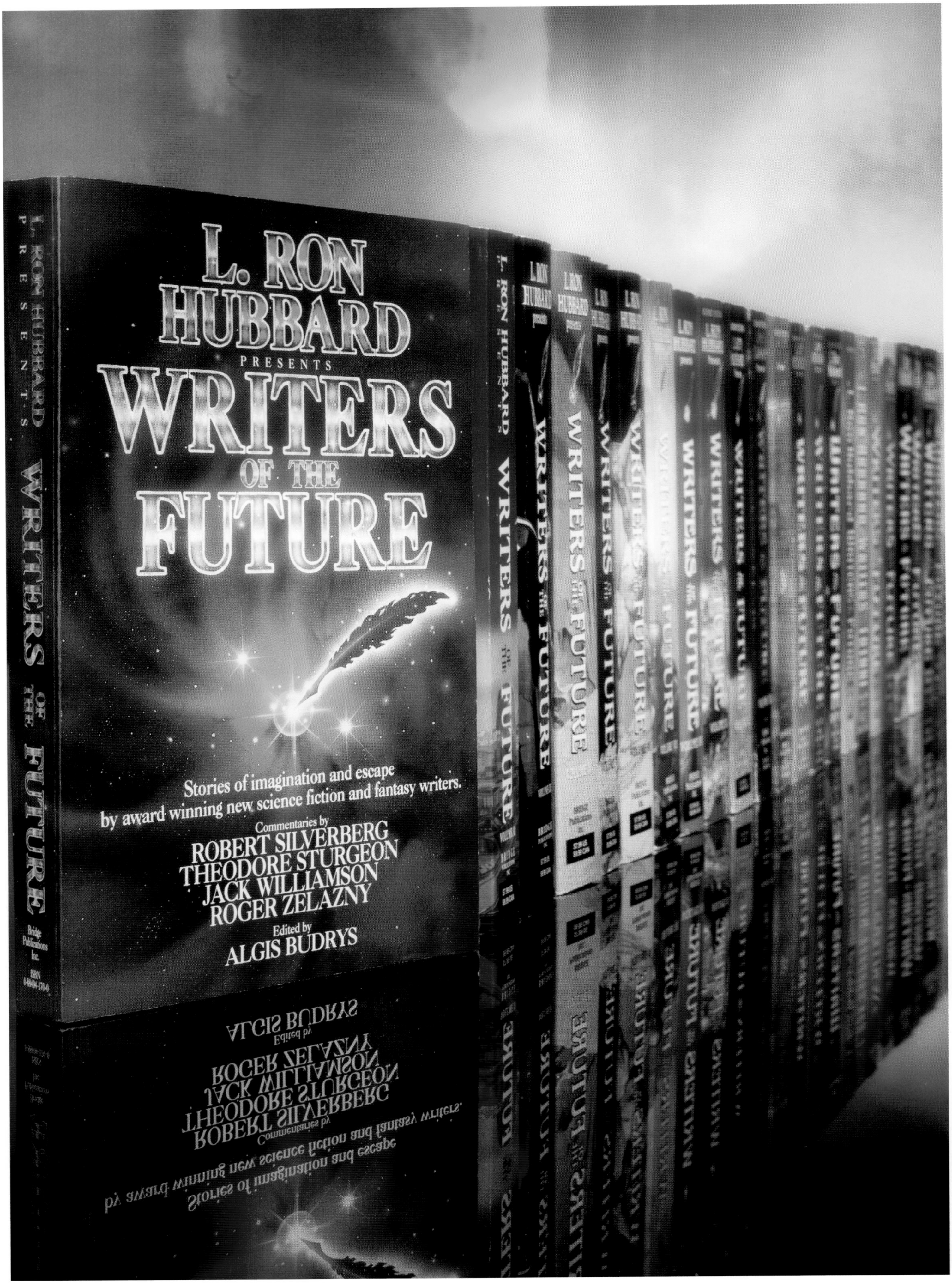

# L. RON HUBBARD

### PRESENTS

# WRITERS OF THE FUTURE

Stories of imagination and escape
by award-winning new science fiction and fantasy writers.

Commentaries by
ROBERT SILVERBERG
THEODORE STURGEON
JACK WILLIAMSON
ROGER ZELAZNY

Edited by
ALGIS BUDRYS

Bridge Publications Inc.

ISBN 0-88404-176-0

ALGIS BUDRYS
Edited by

ROGER ZELAZNY
JACK WILLIAMSON
THEODORE STURGEON
ROBERT SILVERBERG
Commentaries by

Stories of imagination and escape
by award-winning new science fiction and fantasy writers.

# Writers & Illustrators of the Future

If *BATTLEFIELD EARTH* AND *MISSION EARTH* were the final L. Ron Hubbard novels, those works by no means comprised the end of his lifelong commitment to the literary arts. Years earlier, as president of the American Fiction Guild's New York chapter, he had ceaselessly lobbied on behalf of new writers: working to see them admitted as novices into the Guild's professional ranks, generating instructional articles for the various professional journals and otherwise helping the unpublished author take his place in what was traditionally a closed marketplace.

Then in late 1983, declaring, "I initiated a means for new and budding writers to have a chance for their creative efforts to be seen and acknowledged," he announced his *Writers of the Future Contest*. Founded in the name of discovering and encouraging new writers of speculative fiction, the Writers of the Future Award has become the genre's most prestigious award of its kind. Indeed, it is now the largest, most successful and demonstrably most influential vehicle for budding creative talent in the world of contemporary fiction. Reflective of Mr. Hubbard's concern for the aspiring artist, the only entry prohibition is that candidates must not have been professionally published. To ensure professional expertise in the selection

of winners, past and present judges represent some of the greatest names in speculative fiction, including: Larry Niven, Orson Scott Card, Robert Silverberg, Frank Herbert, Jerry Pournelle, Frederik Pohl, Jack Williamson and Anne McCaffrey.

Given Mr. Hubbard originally began his career in an era when popular fiction typically carried elaborate illustrations, it was only fitting he would also inspire the companion *Illustrators of the Future Contest*. Founded to encourage the speculative fiction artist, it provides winning contestants with both cash awards and publication in the annual *L. Ron Hubbard Presents Writers of the Future* anthology.

Those taking awards at the Writers of the Future Contest have left an indelible imprint in the field. That anthology, incidentally, is the top-selling work of its kind and a reliable springboard to the publication of further works. In evidence thereof, Writers of

The Golden Pen Award (left) and Golden Brush Award annually bestowed to the grand prize winners of the Writers of the Future and Illustrators of the Future Contests

the Future contestants have filled American bookshelves with nearly a thousand trendsetting novels and 3,500 short stories. Winners of the illustrators contest have similarly graced well over a thousand publications with imaginative images and placed upwards of a million prints in the public domain. Contest winners have further collected well over fifty premier awards from

elsewhere across the field, including numerous *Hugos* and *Nebulas*—not to mention *National Book Awards* and grants from the National Endowment for the Arts. Indeed and in full, with better than a third of all Writers of the Future winners advancing to professionally published careers, here is exactly what L. Ron Hubbard intended when inaugurating his contest for new and budding authors and illustrators. ▪

# Literary Legacy

"The artist is looked upon to start things," wrote L. Ron Hubbard at the outset of his contest, "The artist injects the spirit of life into the culture." Although he had been speaking of the authors to follow, these same sentiments certainly applied to himself. Today there are some three hundred million L. Ron Hubbard fiction and nonfiction books in circulation. As new generations discover his works, that figure will only continue to grow. But in either case, the mark has been made. As Professor of English and Foreign Languages, Stephen V. Whaley declared, "Without a doubt, L. Ron Hubbard is one of the most prolific and influential writers of the twentieth century."

In evidence of exactly that, the larger body of his works has been honored with awards from such literary organizations as the French National Federation for Culture, the French Academy of Arts, the European Committee of Prestige and an Award of Excellence from the United Nations Society of Writers. Also in recognition of L. Ron Hubbard's literary legacy is a *Charlie Award* from the Hollywood Arts Council and which, in fact, marked the inauguration of an entirely new award category to acknowledge what the Writers of the Future spells for imaginative fiction as a whole. In further evidence of Mr. Hubbard's literary stature stands his extraordinarily vast and diverse body of readers—quite literally from every conceivable corner of society across nearly a hundred nations and in every major language of Earth. Finally, and yet again bespeaking of the future, there are the scores of colleges and universities where students study his work and thereby strive, as he himself so passionately phrased it:

*"To write, write and then write some more. And never to allow weariness, lack of time, noise, or any other thing to throw me off my course."* ■

*For the complete body of information on Mr. Hubbard's literary legacy see the L. Ron Hubbard Series editions on Writer: The Shaping of Popular Fiction; Literary Correspondence Letters & Journals; and Poet/Lyricist: The Aesthetics of Verse.*

# Music Maker

ALTHOUGH MR. HUBBARD NEVER COUNTED HIMSELF AS A professional musician in the strictest sense, his musical accomplishments are by no means insignificant. A radio balladeer in the 1930s, he once held a slot Arthur Godfrey would later fill, he would continue to compose and perform through the remainder of his life.

In the 1970s, he organized, instructed and orchestrated several performing groups and from this work comes a number of incisive essays, including: his analysis of Country Western, Flamenco, traditional Oriental and even Rock music (which he correctly observed was growing increasingly primitive). Notable among his own compositions through the period are his innovative blends of modern jazz, reggae and calypso, as well as his modern utilization of traditional Spanish and Oriental forms. Also highly innovative is his delineation of what he termed "the laws of proportionate sound," wherein similar instruments of slightly different timbre were employed to overcome the long troublesome problem of instrumental cancellation, i.e., the sound of one instrument "wiping out" another regardless of volume. Although professionals have devised various

remedies, Mr. Hubbard was factually the first to both dissect the problem and define its solution. The net effect of such musical innovation is most impressive. Indeed, wrote a critic of the day, L. Ron Hubbard solves "a problem the likes of which Buddy Rich and even Woody Herman failed to do. That is, focus the energy of a combo in a big band, a feat which is like harnessing the atom."

The next L. Ron Hubbard offering was likewise both imaginative and innovative: a soundtrack for his bestselling novel, *Battlefield Earth*. Appropriately entitled *Space Jazz,* the album was the first to fully utilize the capabilities of the Fairlight Computer Musical Instrument. In particular, he employed the Fairlight to "sample" natural sounds and then presented those sounds through the keyboard as notes. Thus *Space Jazz* becomes a "tapestry" of gunshots, tinkling bottles and the like germane to the story—but all woven into percussion and rhythm. In all, the album features thirteen L. Ron Hubbard compositions, inspired by characters and significant events from his novel. The album additionally features performances by jazz legends Chick Corea and Stanley Clarke as well as the equally legendary Rolling Stones pianist Nicky Hopkins.

Given the biting satire inherent in the novel, Mr. Hubbard's next work, *Mission Earth,* the album, is an appropriately hard-rock statement. The featured artist is an ever-innovative Edgar Winter and the album's single, "Cry Out," was later adopted by environmentalists as a marching song to halt unchecked pollution. But the album is particularly remembered for L. Ron Hubbard's then wholly original use of "counter-rhythms"—being a *second* rhythm underlying the drums and typically at a lower pitch. Hence: "*This counter-rhythm would surge*

exactly in the same way as the rest of the beat." The result, as Winter himself remarked: "it slowly began to dawn on us that we were creating a whole new sound with a full symphonic backdrop to a surging rock ensemble."

The final L. Ron Hubbard album, *The Road to Freedom,* reflects Mr. Hubbard's oft repeated maxim, "Music is indeed the Universal Language." In this case, he employs it to convey fundamental truths contained in Scientology. In that respect, the work stands as religious music in Scientology style. Again, the album features performances by Scientologists from the entertainment industry. *The Road to Freedom* further features a vocal performance by Mr. Hubbard himself on a final song, very appropriately entitled "Thank You for Listening." ▪

*For the complete body of information on Mr. Hubbard's musical legacy see the L. Ron Hubbard Series edition, Music Maker: Composer & Performer.*

# Photographer

PHOTOGRAPHY, AS L. RON HUBBARD WAS FOND OF POINTING out, means "Light writing," and given the way in which his photographs communicate, the phrase is entirely apt.

A keen student of the camera through his youth, his career effectively began in the late 1920s with a series of celebrated studies taken through the course of travels in Asia and the South Pacific. The work was squarely professional and ultimately purchased by *National Geographic*. Returning to the United States, he continued on a firmly professional track as both a photojournalist for local newspapers and, on a freelance basis, for a variety of national publications. Most notable among the latter was his work for the air-enthusiast publication *The Sportsman Pilot*.

With the commencement of his formal writing career in 1933, Mr. Hubbard's photographic work tended to take a back seat. Nevertheless, his later years still regularly found him behind the camera for work that included promotional photographs for various European bodies and much acclaimed landscapes of southern England (the latter eventually selected from among 3,300 entries for the International Photography Exhibition in Nantes). Mr. Hubbard's photographs from these years were also selected for display at the Versailles Salon International d'Art Photographique and subsequently saw publication in the L. Ron Hubbard photographic calendars.

In 1975, he continued such work on the island of Curaçao in the Netherlands Antilles, where in a matter of a few days of his arrival it was reported: "Mr. Hubbard with his professional acuteness gets the shots he wants, one after another at a production rate of more than 7,000 photographs since he first started taking photographs here in Curaçao."

Returning to the United States in 1976 to establish a home in Southern California, L. Ron Hubbard's

photographic career took another turn entirely: training students of photography. From this instructional work came his delineation of all vital steps the photographer must take to ensure a successful shot—including the often-neglected preliminary of envisioning or preconceiving the picture. Or as an alternative, he advised photographers learn to immediately recognize a picture. In either case—and herein lay the common denominator of all L. Ron Hubbard's artistic work—photographers must learn to "make the picture *talk*." As a part of the instruction process, all students were privileged with a personal L. Ron Hubbard review of their photographs. In addition to the more conventional points

The L. Ron Hubbard Camera Room housing a collection of photographic equipment assembled from some sixty years of "writing with light"

of composition and lighting, he typically continued to stress that very key matter of communication: What, if anything, did the picture say? Also from this instructional period came his benchmark testing procedures for both equipment and film, and his clarification of that long-misunderstood subject, composition.

Today, the definitive body of his photographic work has been carefully assembled in the L. Ron Hubbard Series edition, *Photographer: Writing with Light* and *Images of a*

*Lifetime: A Photographic Biography.* In all, more than 600 photographs are presented, from his earliest shots with a simple Kodak Brownie to his later work in Southern California. Included, of course, are several selections from his famed China series, his award-winning shots of the English countryside and all else that defined the man's work as "writing with light." ■

# Filmmaker

"EVERY SEPARATE SECTOR OF ARTISTIC CREATIONS," WROTE Mr. Hubbard, "has its own basic rules." By way of example, he cited writing and painting but was particularly addressing members of the cinematographic unit he had established for the production of Scientology training films. His involvement in the field says much about the

man. Although he had only informally stood behind the camera through his Hollywood days in the 1930s, by the spring of 1979 there was literally no aspect of the subject he had not studied. In evidence thereof stand eleven basic texts on the subject he drafted through the course of training film crews in Southern California.

These texts represent a clean distillation of the filmmaking process and the fundamentals of lighting, set design, editing, costumes and more. Of special note are Mr. Hubbard's writings on acting—a field that, because it mirrors life itself, obviously intrigued him. In particular, he objected to psychology's intrusion into the art as advocated by the Stanislavsky Method and the popular notion that the actor must "graft" his own psychological suffering onto a role with what has been perplexingly described as "a free

flow of psychic energy from [the] unconscious." Regardless of meaning, it is a long and emotionally painful process. To the writer and real actor, Mr. Hubbard declared, such methods were disastrous and, in fact, "directly contrary to the role of an artist."

His solution was a series of eighteen instructional essays on the art of acting. All told, those essays comprise a wholly new statement on performance and revolve around the idea that an actor is one who simply conceives how his character would be—how he would walk, speak, gesture—and molds his role accordingly. Subsequent notes on the subject further defined the use of expression, diction, gestures—and very importantly—the employment of L. Ron Hubbard's discovery of the *Emotional Tone Scale,* which delineated the full range of 59 emotions a being can assume.

The L. Ron
Hubbard Film
Room with
displays of his
cinematographic,
audio recording
and mixing
equipment.
Also on display
are his classic
shooting scripts
from Hollywood's
Golden Age.

Drawing upon his many years of experience in radio and recording—from his work as a radio performer in the 1930s to his hands-on recording of filmed dialogue and live mixing of musical performances—Mr. Hubbard's recommendations relating to sound recording are no less significant. In the main, he declared, the field was rife with conflicting opinions and uncodified data. Indeed, he wrote, "There are no textbooks concerning the *operator* side of the field of sound recording, mixing and transferring." Consequently, "I have undertaken to make available, where needed, precise and useful data on the subject of operation of sound equipment." Today, it is no exaggeration to describe the final implementation of L. Ron Hubbard's discoveries and technology on sound recording, mixing, copying and transferring as unmatched in terms of care and quality. This sound technology, dubbed *Clearsound*

and exclusively utilized by the Church of Scientology's Golden Era Productions, has led to an excellence in recording and reproduction that surpasses virtually all industry standards.

Moreover and all told, the thousand-plus pages of Mr. Hubbard's instructional materials on the filmmaking process have thus far proven instrumental in the production of well over 2,000 educational films, documentaries and award-winning public service announcements.

In that regard, there now stands an entire body of filmic work bearing the stamp of L. Ron Hubbard and reflecting what has legitimately been described as the single most definitive statement on the making of memorable films. ■

# Author Services, Inc.

MEETING POPULAR DEMAND FOR THE ARTISTIC works of L. Ron Hubbard is his literary and creative representative, Author Services, Inc. As an umbrella agency, Author Services oversees the distribution of all Mr. Hubbard's creative properties. In that capacity and most significantly, 1986 saw the

agency embarking on a republication schedule for all early L. Ron Hubbard fiction and all remaining unpublished tales. *Fear* and *Final Blackout*, among the first to see reprint, promptly soared to bestseller lists in a telling restatement of popularity from fifty years earlier, as did *Buckskin Brigades* and *To the Stars*.

But what amounts to the mother lode of the L. Ron Hubbard literary legacy and the catalyst of a Pulp Fiction Renaissance is *Stories from the Golden Age*. Featuring original artwork and comprising more than eighty volumes, here are 150 classic tales positively shimmering with pulp magic. In consequence comes what is indeed a rebirth of pulp fiction with an international fan base now including fervent readers all over Africa, Asia and Arabia. Also in consequence comes a worldview and retrospective view of an author *Publishers Weekly* described as "one

of the greatest literary figures of the century." While if only to cap it with an appropriate flourish, with *Stories from the Golden Age*, L. Ron Hubbard additionally earns three Guinness World Records as *Most Published Author, Most Translated Author* and *Author with Most Audio Books*.

There is substantially more. Under Author Services stewardship comes a collection of L. Ron Hubbard audiobooks that have likewise earned an unprecedented place in the annals of twenty-first-century publishing. To be sure, here were the first audiobook presentations to feature a total "sonic-landscape" enveloping listeners in a total literary environment—replete with howling wind, cracking whips, gunshots and cries of vengeance, as the case may be. Here, too, were the first audiobooks to feature scores of actors

*Top*
The L. Ron Hubbard Library at Author Services, Inc., with shelves bearing more than 200 LRH titles and translated foreign editions from nearly a hundred nations

*Below left*
Writers of the Future Hall presenting an array of novels, novelettes and story collections from contest winners who went on to enjoy professionally published careers

in a multicast reading that captures the synergy of a live reading and thus effectively replicate Golden Age of Radio presentations of the 1930s. Moreover, when factoring in the entire library of L. Ron Hubbard audiobooks—including both *Battlefield Earth* and *Mission Earth*—one is looking at production exceeding all industry records. To be sure, *Mission Earth* alone stands as the longest audiobook ever recorded. And when coupled with all 216 audiobook titles, the final tally comes to an unprecedented 463 hours of superlative unabridged multicast audiobook performances.

Similarly presenting a total literary environment are Author Services theatrical readings of L. Ron Hubbard tales. Frequently featuring original performers from the audiobook cast, live readings likewise inspire an international following from as far afield as Malaysia, Australia and Denmark. The point here: What was once described as a "Great American Pulp Movement" is no longer a solely American phenomena. Hence, the L. Ron Hubbard tales in languages as varied as Chinese Mandarin, Malay, Thai and Dutch. Hence, too, a body of pulp fiction that is once again synonymous with *popular* fiction. And hence, an author who indeed taught us what creative writing is finally all about. ∎

*Below right*
Evoking radio dramas from the 1930s are live readings of L. Ron Hubbard tales at the Author Services Golden Age Theater in Hollywood, California

Some of the more than 4,000 awards, proclamations and recognitions bestowed upon LRH to acknowledge a lifetime of creative and humanitarian service. Included are awards for his revolutionary work in the fields of drug rehabilitation, education, criminal reform, moral resurgence and the arts.

*"I like to help others and count it as my*

*greatest pleasure in life to see a person free*

*himself of the shadows which darken his days.*

*"These shadows look so thick to him and*

*weigh him down so that when he finds they*

*are shadows and that he can see through*

*them, walk through them and be again in the*

*sun, he is enormously delighted. And I am*

*afraid I am just as delighted as he is."*

L. Ron Hubbard

# Epilogue

Philosopher, humanitarian, author, artist, educator and administrator—L. Ron Hubbard served us in a myriad of ways. In turn, he is quite literally viewed by millions worldwide as Mankind's greatest friend: by those now literate, by those now drug-free, by those who used his work to reclaim their honor and self-respect, by those who enjoy newfound prosperity, morality and the unmatched joy of artistic creation.

Yet what Mr. Hubbard ultimately provided in the name of uplifting humanity is found in the more than 75 million words of recorded lectures, books and related writings comprising the totality of Dianetics and Scientology. If this profile has barely touched upon those subjects, he nonetheless ensured that greater legacy is available to all who would avail themselves of it. True, this road to eternal freedom demands some commitment, some determination. But he never expected one to walk it blindly or without inspection. Rather and very simply:

*"This is the track of knowing how*

*to know. Travel it and see."*

# APPENDIX

# GLOSSARY

## A

**abiding:** continuing without change; enduring; lasting. Page 4.

**aboriginal:** characteristic of groups of people that have existed from the earliest days; existing from the earliest known times. Page 4.

**acuity:** the ability to understand quickly and clearly; perceptiveness of mind. Page 105.

**adage:** a traditional saying expressing a common experience or observation; a proverb. Page 19.

**aesthetics:** the study or theory of beauty and responses to it; specifically, the branch of philosophy dealing with art, its creative sources, its forms and its effects. Page 135.

**afield:** distant from a place, area or the like. Page 163.

**airy:** like air in its (apparently) intangible or empty character; not based on reality. Page 27.

**Alaskan Radio Experimental Expedition:** a 1,500-mile (2,400-kilometer) voyage conducted to provide data for correct mapping of the coastline between the northwestern shores of the continental US and the southern part of Alaska. The expedition resulted in photographs and navigational information to correct the previously mischarted coastline. Page 41.

**Aleutian islanders:** a Native North American people of southwestern coastal Alaska and the *Aleutian Islands,* a chain of islands off southwest Alaska. These islands separate the Bering Sea to the north from the Pacific Ocean to the south. Page 42.

**American Fiction Guild:** a national organization of magazine fiction writers and novelists in the United States in the 1930s. L. Ron Hubbard was the president of the New York chapter in 1936. Page 34.

**American University:** a private university in Washington, DC, founded in 1893. It offers courses in a broad range of fields, including arts and sciences, communications, public affairs, business administration and law. Page 99.

**Anglican Church:** any Christian church that follows the teachings of the *Church of England,* the national church of England that has the king or queen of England as its head. Page 118.

**annotation(s):** a note added to a text, diagram, chart or the like, giving explanation or comment. Page 3.

**anthology:** a book or other collection of selected writings by various authors, usually in the same literary form or the same period or on the same subject. Page 145.

**antisubmarine:** of or relating to the various methods employed in war to detect and fight enemy submarines, including locating with a device that picks up reflected pulses of sound and fighting with various explosive devices. Page 5.

**apathies:** attitudes or feelings of apathy manifested by a lack of feeling or emotion; absences of interest or concern. Page 7.

**aphorism:** a succinct statement expressing a general truth or an opinion. Page 63.

***Apollo:*** from the late 1960s through the mid-1970s, the upper-management activities for all Churches of Scientology over the world were conducted from a fleet of ships, the main vessel being the *Apollo.* The vessel also served as L. Ron Hubbard's home and center for his many research activities. Page 75.

***Argosy:*** an American fiction magazine published by the Frank A. Munsey Company, first produced in the late 1800s. Containing science fiction, fantasy and other genres. Page 137.

**arranging:** the action of choosing the instruments and adding chording (harmonious combinations of three or more notes played simultaneously) and backup to a melody. Page 78.

**array:** a large group, number or quantity (of things). Page 23.

**arrayed:** placed or positioned properly, as for effective use. Page 109.

**associate professor:** an academic ranking immediately below full professor, the highest rank. Page 99.

***Astounding Science Fiction:*** a magazine founded in 1930, which featured adventure stories and, later, science fiction. Page 41.

***Athena:*** a Sea Org ship, originally named *Avon River.* A converted fishing vessel, *Athena* was approximately 145 feet (44 meters) long and steam driven. Page 75.

**auditing:** also called *processing,* the application of Dianetics or Scientology techniques (called *processes*). Page 9.

**auspices of, under the:** with the approval or support of. Page 41.

**axiomatic:** based on or having to do with *axioms,* statements of natural laws on the order of those of the physical sciences. Page 71.

**axioms:** statements of natural laws on the order of those of the physical sciences. Page 50.

# B

**back seat, take a:** occupy a secondary position. Page 153.

**balladeer:** a person who sings *ballads,* any light, simple song, especially one of sentimental or romantic character. Page 29.

**barnstorming:** in the early days of aviation, touring (the country) giving short airplane rides, exhibitions of stunt flying, etc. This term comes from the use of barns as hangars. Page 2.

**barometer:** something that indicates a change. Literally, a *barometer* is an instrument that measures changes in atmospheric pressure as a signal of changing weather. Page 129.

**bear, bring to:** exert an influence on, so as to cause an effect or attain something desired. Page 6.

**behest:** an earnest or strongly worded request. Page 83.

**beleaguered:** surrounded with an army so as to prevent escape; hemmed in. Page 44.

**benchmark:** pertaining to or used as a standard of excellence, achievement, etc., against which anything similar must be measured or judged. Page 110.

**bereft:** lacking in something desirable or necessary. Page 113.

**besieged:** flooded with large numbers of questions, requests and the like. Page 6.

**bespeaking of:** speaking of or showing beforehand. Page 147.

**bestow:** give or present something to someone. Page 145.

**big band:** a jazz or dance band having usually sixteen to twenty players, including sections of different instruments (for example, rhythm, brass, etc.) and performing arrangements of jazz, popular dance music, etc. Page 149.

**biochemical:** of or concerning the chemical substances present in living organisms and the changes, reactions, etc., related to the chemical processes that happen in living things. Page 106.

**Blackfeet:** a group of Native North American peoples including the Blackfeet of Montana and several tribes now living in Canada. This group controlled areas that were fought over by fur traders in the 1800s. Page 3.

**Black Mask:** one of the best-known and admired pulp fiction magazines. Originally an all-around publication that included detective, westerns and aviation stories, *Black Mask* later focused on detective fiction, publishing stories by top writers in the field. Page 137.

**blood brother:** either one of two men or boys who have sworn mutual loyalty and friendship, typically by a ritual or ceremony involving a superficial cut in the skin and the mingling (mixing) of each other's blood. Page 3.

**brigade(s):** in the Canadian and US fur trade, a convoy of canoes, sleds, wagons or pack animals used to supply trappers during the eighteenth and nineteenth centuries. Page 140.

**British Columbia:** a province in western Canada on the Pacific coast. Page 3.

**budding:** beginning to show a particular degree of understanding, skill, proficiency or the like; developing. Page 145.

**Bureau of Marine Inspection and Navigation:** an agency responsible for examination and licensing of marine officers and for inspection and enforcement of marine safety laws. Originally the bureau was part of the Department of Commerce. The licensing function was later assigned to the Coast Guard. (*Marine* means of or related to navigation, shipping or the sea.) *See also* **Department of Commerce.** Page 42.

**Burks, Arthur J.:** (1898–1974) American writer whose enormous output for the pulps included aviation, detective, adventure and horror stories. Page 137.

**Burroughs, Edgar Rice:** (1875–1950) American writer best known for creating the character Tarzan in his novel *Tarzan of the Apes,* which appeared in 1914. Burroughs also wrote science fiction novels. Along with his twenty-six Tarzan stories, he wrote a total of more than seventy books. Page 34.

**byroad:** a side road or a minor road. Used figuratively to mean a course of action, investigation, etc., that is minor or less important when compared to others. Page 8.

# C

**calypso:** a musical style of West Indian origin, influenced by jazz, usually having improvised lyrics reflecting current interests. Page 149.

**canon:** a list of literary works considered to be permanently established as being of the highest quality. Page 141.

**Card, Orson Scott:** (1951– ) American author of science fiction, fantasy, poetry, plays and scripts. His speculative fiction novels have earned him numerous awards including the Nebula and Hugo. Card is a professor of literature and writing and has authored two books on writing. He has also been a Writers of the Future judge since 1994 and served as an instructor at the first Writers of the Future workshop in 1986. Page 145.

**catalyst:** something that stimulates a reaction, development or change. Page 118.

**cellular:** having to do with a *cell,* the smallest structural unit of an organism that is capable of independent functioning. Page 39.

**Chandler, Raymond:** (1888–1959) American author of crime and detective stories, mostly set in Los Angeles during the 1930s and 1940s. Page 34.

**cinematographic:** relating to, used in or connected with *cinematography,* the art, science and work of lighting and photography in making films. Page 157.

**cite(d):** mention, especially as an example of what one is saying. Page 10.

**Classification and Gradation Chart:** also called the *Bridge,* the precise steps of auditing and training that one advances through to reach one's native potentials. *Classification* refers to training and the fact that certain actions are required, or skills attained, before an individual is classified for a particular training level and allowed onto the next class. *Gradation* refers to the gradual improvement that occurs in Scientology auditing. Page 73.

**Clear:** a being who no longer has his own reactive mind. He is a person who is not affected by aberration (any deviation or departure from rationality). He is rational in that he forms the best possible solutions he can on the data he has and from his viewpoint. Page 7.

**cloistered:** secluded or sheltered from the harsh realities of life, similar to living in a *cloister,* literally, a place where people live a life of religious seclusion and contemplation. Page 17.

**combo:** a small jazz or dance band having usually from three to six players. Page 149.

**commissioned:** given a *commission,* a document conferring authority to officers in the army, navy and other military services, issued by the president of the United States. Page 44.

**common denominator:** something common to or characteristic of a number of people, things, situations, etc.; shared characteristic. Page 5.

**composition:** the arrangement of elements within a photograph so that they are displayed in their most pleasing arrangement as a harmonious, well-balanced whole. Page 78.

**Compton:** a city and suburb of Los Angeles, California. Page 101.

**compunction:** a strong uneasiness caused by a sense of guilt. Page 113.

**Computer Musical Instrument (CMI):** a computer-based musical instrument with a keyboard like that of a piano, capable of recording any sound from natural or electronic sources, such as animals, the wind, a tape machine or other sound source. Sounds recorded into it would conform to musical notes, playable by means of its keyboard like any other musical note. The CMI was also called the *Fairlight,* a name given it by its creator, who named it after a ferryboat in Sydney, Australia. Page 149.

**conception:** an idea of what something or someone is like or a basic understanding of a situation or a principle. Page 102.

**conglomeration:** an accumulation or mass of dissimilar materials or elements. Page 97.

**Congolese:** of or relating to the people, culture, etc., of the Democratic Republic of the Congo. Formerly a colony of Belgium, the country became independent in 1960 and has experienced much turmoil from civil wars. Page 119.

**contemplative:** given to *contemplation,* the action of thinking or considering something; theoretical as opposed to practical. Page 1.

**control group:** a group of individuals not using some procedure as compared with those who do use it, created to correctly compare and contrast the results of a test. Page 101.

**convoy:** a group of ships traveling together and accompanied by a protecting escort. Page 44.

**cornerstone:** a fundamental element or part of something; basic; essential. Literally, a cornerstone is a stone that forms part of the corner of the foundation of a building. Page 1.

**corollary:** that follows from or derives naturally from a circumstance or phenomenon; resulting. Page 107.

**court:** the residence of a king, queen or other high dignitary; palace. Page 4.

**Creston, California:** a rural community in central California, known for its horse ranches. Page 81.

**Curaçao:** an island in the southern Caribbean Sea, lying off the coast of Venezuela. The island, an autonomous country within the Kingdom of the Netherlands, is a popular tourist destination. Page 78.

**cursory:** going rapidly over something, without becoming involved in details. Page 139.

**cusp of, from the:** at or during a time of transition, such as the moment of, or just before, a major change or event. Page 135.

**cyberspace iniquity:** abuse of free speech to spread falsehoods and hatred anonymously or otherwise through the Internet. Page 87.

# D

**daredevil:** a person who shows a carefree disregard for risk or danger, especially by performing dangerous stunts. Page 29.

**date coincident:** happening or existing at the same time. Page 119.

**decree:** a formal and authoritative order, especially one having the force of law. Page 125.

**decreed:** commanded (something); ordered or assigned authoritatively. Page 141.

**decry:** speak out against strongly and openly; denounce. Page 61.

**deficit(s):** the amount by which money spent or owed is greater than money earned in a particular period of time. Page 125.

**definitive:** having a fixed and final form; providing a solution or final answer; satisfying all requirements. Page 7.

**deleterious:** harmful to health or well-being; injurious. Page 76.

**denomination:** a religious group united under a common faith with a specific name and organization. Page 78.

**Department of Commerce:** a department of the United States Government established in 1903 with the purpose to promote the nation's economic development and technological advancement. During the early 1900s, one of the department's functions was issuing licenses to *masters,* those in command of nonnaval ships. This function was later assigned to the US Coast Guard. Page 44.

**derivation symbols:** any symbols, abbreviations or the like used in presenting data about a *derivation,* the origin and development of a word showing how it has arrived at its current form and meaning. These could include symbols such as + (to show that a word is made up of two parts) or < (to show that a word comes from an earlier word) or abbreviations of names of languages, etc. Page 100.

**diagrammatic:** in the form of an explanatory drawing or chart. Page 125.

**Dianetics:** Dianetics is a forerunner and substudy of Scientology. Dianetics means "through the mind" or "through the soul" (from Greek *dia,* through, and *nous,* mind or soul). Dianetics is further defined as what the mind or soul is doing to the body. Page 1.

**Dianetics: The Evolution of a Science:** an article originally written by L. Ron Hubbard for a national magazine, published in advance of the release of *Dianetics: The Modern Science of Mental Health* and detailing how he arrived at the breakthrough discoveries of Dianetics. Page 48.

**Dianetics: The Original Thesis:** a book written by L. Ron Hubbard in 1948, detailing the first formal record of his research and discoveries on the structure and function of the human mind. Page 6.

**diction:** way of speaking or pronouncing words. Page 157.

**die-hard:** resistant to any kind of change and reluctant to give up habits, beliefs or attitudes. Page 109.

**dimension:** any of the component aspects of a particular situation, etc., especially one newly discovered. Page 3.

**discipline:** a branch of knowledge or learning. Page 4.

**distillation:** something that has been refined by having essential elements discovered or brought to view. Page 99.

**doctrine:** a body of ideas, particularly in religion, taught to people as true or correct. Page 10.

**doled out:** given out in small portions. Page 4.

**downs:** treeless, hilly areas with fairly smooth slopes usually covered with grass, particularly as found in southern England. Page 64.

**drive-by shooting:** an attack on a person, group or building carried out by an individual or individuals from a moving vehicle. Drive-by shootings are employed by gang members often in revenge murders. Page 113.

**drive(s):** an inner urge that stimulates activity; energy and initiative. Page 115.

**Dr. P.H.:** an abbreviation for *Doctor of Public Health*. The field of *public health* includes areas such as health education, the prevention and control of diseases, environmental safety and pollution control. Page 107.

**Dunedin, Florida:** a city and winter resort area in western Florida, on the Gulf of Mexico. Page 78.

**dynamic:** full of energy, enthusiasm and a sense of purpose, and able both to get things going and to get things done. Page 2.

**Dynamic Principle of Existence:** the lowest common denominator of existence—the discovery by L. Ron Hubbard that the goal of life can be considered to be infinite survival. Man, as a life form, can be demonstrated to obey in all his actions and purposes the one command, *"Survive!"* It is not a new thought that Man is surviving. It is a new thought that Man is motivated only by survival. Page 29.

# E

**Eagle Scout:** a Boy Scout who has reached the highest level of attainment in various tests of skill and endurance. Page 23.

**earthquake, Los Angeles:** a 6.7 magnitude earthquake that occurred approximately 20 miles (31 kilometers) from downtown Los Angeles, California, in 1994. It resulted in more than fifty deaths and many billions in property damage. Damage occurred up to 85 miles (125 kilometers) from the center of the earthquake. Page 118.

**Eastern Cape:** a province in southeastern South Africa, on the Indian Ocean. Page 118.

**echelon:** a level, as in a steplike arrangement or order. An *echelon* is one of a series in a field of activity. Page 50.

**eclipsed:** blocked or obscured, as if by being covered over. Literally, an eclipse occurs, for example, when the Sun is hidden from view because the Moon comes between it and the observer. Page 97.

**edge on it, not to put too fine an:** expressing (something) in a blunt, direct way. Page 101.

**efficacy:** the capacity for producing a desired result or effect; effectiveness. Page 7.

**Elizabeth, New Jersey:** a city in northeastern New Jersey, USA, which was the location of the first Hubbard Dianetic Research Foundation, 1950–1951. Page 48.

***El Tiempo:*** a daily newspaper published in Bogotá, Colombia, and having several regional editions. With its national distribution, *El Tiempo* is the largest newspaper in the country. It was founded in 1911. Page 119.

**embracive:** including the entirety of something, so as to be complete. Page 114.

**Emotional Tone Scale:** a scale that shows the successive emotional tones a person can experience. By *tone* is meant the momentary or continuing emotional state of a person. Emotions such as fear, anger, grief, enthusiasm and others which people experience are shown on this graduated scale. A Tone Scale tells you how people behave. If people are at a certain level on the Tone Scale, then they behave in a certain way and you can predict how they will behave. Page 157.

**end, to that:** for that purpose or reason. Page 9.

**engender:** bring into existence; produce. Page 61.

**engrams:** mental recordings of pain and unconsciousness. Page 7.

**enjoined:** urged in an authoritative way; directed. Page 41.

**ensconced:** established in a place or position. Page 24.

**enthralling:** intensely interesting; thrilling. Page 4.

**environmentalist:** a person who is concerned with or advocates the protection of the environment. Page 150.

**Environmental Protection Agency:** an agency of the United States Government established in 1970 and responsible for protecting the environment and maintaining it for future generations. The EPA is supposed to control and reduce air pollution, water pollution and pollution by radiation, pesticides and other toxic substances. Page 106.

**episodic:** divided into, or composed of, closely connected but independent sections. *See also* **serial.** Page 37.

**ethnocentric:** evaluating other cultures according to preconceptions originating in one's own culture. Page 140.

**ethnological:** of or having to do with *ethnology,* the science that analyzes cultures, especially in regard to their historical development and the similarities and dissimilarities between them. Page 141.

**Eufaula, Lake:** a lake in the eastern part of Oklahoma, a state in the south central part of the United States. Page 110.

**evoking:** bringing to mind a memory or feeling, especially from the past. Page 163.

**exacerbated:** made worse, said of an already bad or problematic situation. Page 97.

**"Excalibur":** a philosophic manuscript written by L. Ron Hubbard in 1938. Although unpublished as such, the body of information it contained has since been released in various Dianetics and Scientology materials. Page 5.

**exigencies:** pressing needs or requirements of circumstances; demands. Page 76.

**Explorers Club:** an organization, headquartered in New York and founded in 1904, devoted exclusively to promoting the science of exploration. To further this aim, it provides grants for those who wish to participate in field research projects and expeditions. It has provided logistical support for some of the twentieth century's most daring expeditions. L. Ron Hubbard was a lifetime member of the Explorers Club. Page 41.

**Explorers Club flag:** a flag awarded to active members of the Explorers Club who are in command of, or serving with, expeditions that further the cause of exploration and field science. Since 1918 the Explorers Club flag has been carried on hundreds of expeditions, including those to both North and South Poles, the summit of Mount Everest and the surface of the Moon. Many famous persons in history have carried the Explorers Club flag, including L. Ron Hubbard. Page 75.

**Explorers Journal, The:** a quarterly periodical published since 1921 by the Explorers Club. The club's *Journal* publishes articles and photographs from club members and others on expeditions across the globe. Page 47.

**expunging:** getting rid of something completely, doing away with. Page 107.

**extended:** (of a family group) including parents and children, together with grandparents, aunts, uncles, cousins and sometimes more distant relatives. Page 19.

**extracurricular:** done or happening outside of one's regular study or program of courses. Page 29.

# F

**fabric:** the essential structure of anything; framework. Page 113.

**facsimile:** a copy or representation (of something). Page 93.

**faction(s):** a group that is a minority within a larger group and has specific interests or beliefs that are not always in harmony with the larger group. Page 119.

**factor in:** include something as a relevant element. Page 91.

**fallout, radioactive:** airborne radioactive dust and material shot into the atmosphere by a nuclear explosion which then settles to the ground. *Radioactive* describes a substance that sends out harmful energy in the form of streams of very small particles due to the decay (breaking down) of atoms within the substance. Page 61.

**far-flung:** extended far or to a great distance; remote. Page 2.

**fathomed:** penetrated (something, such as a mystery, puzzle or the like) and understood thoroughly. Page 7.

**fatty tissue:** body tissue containing stored fat that serves as a source of energy; it also cushions and insulates vital organs. Page 105.

**feet, find (one's):** get on one's feet; settle down and develop a grip on one's work, activity, etc. Page 88.

**filmic:** of or relating to motion pictures. Page 159.

**fine an edge on it, not to put too:** expressing (something) in a blunt, direct way. Page 101.

**fire retardant:** a chemical substance, very poisonous to the environment, that has the ability or tendency to slow up or halt the spread of fire. One of the most frequently used fire retardants was accidentally introduced into animal feed in the early 1970s in Michigan (a state in the north central United States), leading to the poisoning of many residents who came in contact with the substance. Page 107.

**first-step program:** any program that seeks to improve social behavior, responsibility and the like, especially for young people who have become involved with crime, by providing the basics as a first step in making such improvements. Page 121.

***Five-Novels Monthly:*** a pulp magazine published from 1928 until the late 1940s. Page 137.

**flamenco:** the Spanish gypsy style of dance (characterized by stamping, clapping, etc.) or music (typically very emotional and mournful). Page 149.

**flashback:** a memory, past incident or event occurring again vividly in one's mind. Specifically, with certain drugs (such as LSD and similar drugs), it is the reemergence of some aspect of the hallucination (which took place while on the drug) in the absence of the drug. The most common form includes altered visual images; wavering, altered borders to visual images; or trails of light. Page 105.

**floundering:** characterized by confused or purposeless motion. Page 125.

**follow suit:** do the same as something else has done; follow an example set. Page 48.

**footage:** a motion picture scene or scenes. Page 31.

**foray:** a new undertaking, especially outside one's usual area. Page 141.

**forefront:** the position of greatest importance or prominence. Page 142.

**fore, to the:** to a position of prominence or importance. Page 101.

**Founding Church:** the Founding Church of Scientology, Washington, DC, established in 1955. A *founding church* is one from which other churches have their origin or derive their authority. Page 58.

**free-flight:** characteristic of any flying, as in a glider, that is not assisted by the power of an engine. Page 29.

**freelance:** of or pertaining to a *freelance,* a writer who writes stories or articles for a number of employers rather than working on a regular salary basis for one employer. Page 29.

**Freudian theory:** also called *psychoanalysis,* a system of mental therapy developed by Sigmund Freud (1856–1939) in Austria in 1894 and which depended upon the following practices for its effects: the patient was encouraged to talk about and recall his childhood years while the practitioner searched for hidden sexual incidents believed by Freud to be the cause of mental ills. The practitioner read significances into all statements and evaluated them for the patient (told him what to think) along sex-related lines. Page 4.

**fringe:** the outer part of something; a part regarded as extreme or not of the mainstream. Page 105.

**fruit:** the result or reward of work or activity. Page 83.

**full-fledged:** with or having full rank, standing or status. Page 3.

**function:** intellectual powers; mental action; thought, as contrasted with *structure,* how something is built or its physical design. Page 6.

# G
_____

**gangbang:** an instance of violence involving members of a criminal gang. Page 113.

**garner:** collect or accumulate, as if by gathering. Page 80.

**Gauteng Province:** a province in northeastern South Africa, location of the city of Johannesburg, the largest city in the country. Page 118.

**genre(s):** a category of artistic composition, as in music or literature, marked by a distinctive style, form or content. Page 41.

**George Washington University:** a private university, founded in 1821, in the city of Washington, DC, and named after the first president of the United States, George Washington (1732–1799). The university has a long history of supporting research in physics and other technical fields. Page 4.

**germane:** closely or significantly related; pertinent. Page 150.

**Glendale, California:** a city in Los Angeles County, southwestern California. Glendale is a residential suburb of Los Angeles. Page 119.

**glider:** a motorless aircraft that is supported in flight by air currents. Gliders are mainly used for sports and recreational purposes. Page 2.

**global village:** the world, especially considered as the home of all nations and peoples living interdependently. Page 114.

**Godfrey, Arthur:** (1903–1983) an American radio and television broadcaster and entertainer. Page 149.

**good as gold:** particularly good or competent, likened to gold, a substance considered to have a superior quality. Page 99.

**graced:** provided with something pleasing, beautiful or the like. Page 146.

**gradient:** done by means of a gradual approach; taking something step by step, level by level, each step or level being, of itself, easily attainable—so that finally, complicated and difficult activities or states can be achieved with relative ease. The term *gradient* also applies to each of the steps taken in such an approach. Page 9.

**graft:** join two things that are dissimilar to each other. Used figuratively. Page 157.

**grammarian:** a person who studies and writes about grammar. Traditionally, *grammar* has been regarded as the system of rules by which words are formed and put together to make sentences. Page 97.

**graphic:** including a number of vivid descriptive details, especially unpleasant ones. Page 113.

**grass-roots:** of, pertaining to or involving the common people in a community who join together and donate their time and support to forward a particular cause. Page 80.

**Great Adventures of Wild Bill Hickok, The:** a 1938 movie serial about the famous lawman of the Old West and his attempts to keep the peace in the frontier. Wild Bill Hickok (1837–1876) was an American frontier army scout, sheriff and gambler whose reputation made him a legend even during his own lifetime. Page 37.

**Greenville, Alabama:** a city in the southern part of Alabama, a state in the southeastern United States. Page 121.

**Guam:** an island in the northwestern Pacific Ocean, a territory of the United States and site of US air and naval bases. Page 24.

**Guinness Book of Records:** a collection of world records (referred to as *Guinness World Records*), both of human achievements as well as of the natural world, which is published as an annual reference book. Page 83.

# H

**Haidas:** a Native North American people living along the coast of British Columbia in Canada, the adjoining Alaskan coast and the islands lying off these areas. Page 42.

**Hammett, Dashiell:** (1894–1961) highly influential American author of detective novels. Drawing on his years of work as a private detective, Hammett began writing in the early 1920s. With his realistic writing style, he created enduringly popular characters and plots, with a number of his best-known works, such as *The Maltese Falcon* (1930), later adapted for film. Page 34.

**hat:** slang for the title and work of a job or position; taken from the fact that in many professions, such as railroading, the type of hat worn is the badge of the job. Page 126.

**haunts:** places frequently visited. Page 31.

**heavy industry:** an industry that requires considerable space and heavy equipment to produce its products. Examples are the iron and steel industry and shipbuilding. Page 130.

**hectographed:** reproduced by means of a *hectograph*, a machine used in the 1940s to '60s, prior to the invention of the modern photocopier, for making many copies of a page of writing or a drawing. Page 6.

**Heinlein, Robert:** (1907–1988) American author considered one of the most important writers of science fiction. Emerging during science fiction's Golden Age (1939–1949), Heinlein went on to write many novels, including the classic *Stranger in a Strange Land* (1961). He won four Hugo Awards and was presented with the first Grand Master Nebula Award for lifetime achievement in science fiction. Page 137.

**Helena:** city and capital of Montana, a state in the northwestern United States bordering on Canada. Page 3.

**helm:** the wheel by which the ship is steered. Page 27.

**helmsman:** the person in charge of steering a ship. The helmsman is stationed at the *helm,* the wheel by which the ship is steered. Page 27.

**heralded:** announced with enthusiasm. Page 142.

**Herbert, Frank:** (1920–1986) acclaimed American science fiction author. While beginning his writing career in the 1950s, he is best known for his bestselling novel *Dune* (1965) and subsequent books in the *Dune Chronicles,* a series that sparked a major motion picture and television series. Herbert also served as a judge in the Writers of the Future Contest. Page 145.

**Herman, Woody:** (1913–1987) American jazz saxophonist, clarinetist and bandleader who for more than fifty years led one of the most consistently popular big bands in jazz. Page 149.

**Hermitage House Publishing:** a publishing firm in New York City, New York, founded in 1947 by editor and publisher Arthur Ceppos (1910–1997). In May 1950, Hermitage House was the first to publish *Dianetics: The Modern Science of Mental Health*. Page 48.

**Hollywood Arts Council:** an organization established to support and promote the arts in Hollywood, California, stemming from "the belief that the arts revitalize people as well as communities." Page 147.

**homestead:** a dwelling with its land and adjoining buildings where a family makes its home. Page 19.

**horticultural:** of or having to do with *horticulture,* the science and art of cultivating flowers, fruits, vegetables or ornamental plants. Page 66.

**Hubbard Association of Scientologists:** during the 1950s and 1960s, the organization that coordinated and provided guidance to all Scientology organizations over the world, served as the central point of dissemination and was the general membership group of the Church. Page 53.

**Hubbard College:** an administration and teaching organization established by L. Ron Hubbard in Wichita, Kansas, in 1951 to advance Dianetics. Page 50.

**Hubbard College (of Administration):** any of the institutions of higher learning that provide training in L. Ron Hubbard's administrative methods. Page 50.

**Hubbard Dianetic Research Foundation:** the first organization of Dianetics, formed in 1950 in Elizabeth, New Jersey, to further Dianetics research and, mainly, to offer training. Page 48.

**hue, other:** another type, kind, form, aspect or the like. Page 114.

**Hugo:** an award for science fiction writing (Hugo Award), initiated in 1953 by the World Science Fiction Society. It is named for influential science fiction editor, writer and inventor Hugo Gernsback (1884–1967), who is credited with starting modern science fiction by founding the first magazine dedicated to this literary field, *Amazing Stories,* in 1926. Page 146.

**hydrogen bomb:** an explosive weapon more powerful than an atomic bomb, that derives its energy from the fusion (combining) of hydrogen atoms. Page 61.

**Hydrographic Office:** a section of the Department of the Navy charged with making hydrographic surveys and publishing charts and other information for naval and commercial vessels, information key to national defense. *Hydrographic* means of or relating to the scientific charting, description and analysis of the physical conditions, boundaries and flow of oceans, lakes, rivers, etc. Page 42.

**hysteria, mass:** a condition in which a large group of people exhibit the same state of extreme or exaggerated emotion, such as excitement, panic, agitation, anxiety. Page 61.

# I

**ideological:** of or relating to *ideology,* a study of the nature and origin of ideas. Page 39.

**imbue:** fill with a feeling or quality. Page 141.

**imparts:** communicates the knowledge of; makes known or reveals. Page 20.

**imperishable:** that cannot disappear or be destroyed; enduring permanently. Page 10.

**impetuously:** on the spur of the moment; impulsively. Page 27.

**impetus:** driving force or motive; impulse. Page 5.

**incisive(ly):** remarkably clear and direct. Page 91.

**incontrovertible:** not open to question or dispute; undeniable. Page 7.

**indelible:** that cannot be eliminated, erased, etc.; permanent. Page 24.

**indigenous:** originating in and characteristic of a particular region or country; native. Page 3.

**ineffable:** incapable of being expressed or described in words; inexpressible. Page 9.

**inextricably:** so closely linked to a person, place or thing that it cannot be considered separately. Page 5.

**infrastructure:** the substructure or underlying foundation needed for the operation of a society or organization. It includes the basic installations and facilities on which the continuance and growth of a community, state, etc., depend. The *social infrastructure* includes among others, the educational, healthcare and welfare systems. The *economic infrastructure* includes the financial system, manufacturing, agriculture, forestry, fisheries, etc. Page 91.

**ingest:** take something (such as food, a liquid or a gas) into the body by swallowing, inhaling or absorbing it. Page 105.

**iniquity, cyberspace:** abuse of free speech to spread falsehoods and hatred anonymously or otherwise through the Internet. Page 87.

**Inside Passage:** a natural protected waterway in northwestern North America, 950 miles (1,500 kilometers) long. It extends along the coast from Seattle, Washington, USA, past British Columbia, Canada, to the southern area of Alaska. The passage is made up of a series of channels running between the mainland and a string of islands on the west that protect the passage from Pacific Ocean storms. Page 41.

**insidious:** operating or proceeding in an inconspicuous or seemingly harmless way but actually with grave effect. Page 105.

**instilled:** having an idea or attitude gradually but firmly established in one's mind. Page 3.

**intergalactic:** of, existing or moving between *galaxies,* any of the numerous large groups of stars and other matter that exist in space as independent systems. Page 139.

**International Photography Exhibition in Nantes:** an international photography exhibit, Salon International de Photographie, held in Nantes, a city in western France. The city is home to one of France's premier museums of fine arts, the Musée des Beaux-Arts, which has one of the most important and varied collections of paintings in the country. Page 153.

**internment camps:** prison camps for the confinement of *prisoners of war,* members of the armed forces who are captured and held by an enemy during war. Page 6.

**irresolution:** an undecided opinion, uncertainty, doubt. Page 7.

J

**Jaipur, Maharajah of:** Sawai Man Singh II (1912–1970), the last ruler of Jaipur in India, before India became a republic in 1950, and owner of Saint Hill Manor during the 1950s. A *maharajah* is a former title used in India for a king or prince, especially the ruler of one of the larger regions. *Jaipur* is a former state in northwestern India, now part of the state of Rajasthan. It is also the name of the chief city of the region, now the capital of Rajasthan. Page 64.

**Johannesburg:** a city located in northeastern South Africa. It is the most important industrial and commercial city in the country. Page 69.

**juvenile hall:** a holding center for juvenile delinquents (persons usually under eighteen years who habitually break the law). It is a secure facility for those who are awaiting court hearings or placement in long-term disciplinary-care programs for committing crimes such as drug possession or robbery. Page 121.

# K

**Kalispell:** a city in northwestern Montana, a state in the northwestern United States bordering on Canada. Page 19.

**kernel:** the central, most important part of something; core; essence. Page 39.

**Ketchikan, Alaska:** a seaport in southeastern Alaska, a transportation and communications center and one of the chief ports on Alaska's Pacific coast. Page 41.

**King, Stephen:** (1947– ) award-winning American novelist and short-story writer and one of the world's bestselling authors. Renowned for his tales of horror, fantasy and the supernatural, King has produced many stories and books that have been made into films. Page 142.

**Kodak Brownie:** a simple, portable, boxlike camera produced in the early 1900s, one of the first to carry roll film (as opposed to the slower single film sheets of earlier cameras). Page 155.

**Kublai Khan:** (1216–1294) military leader of the Mongols, a people living to the north of China. He conquered China, becoming the first non-Chinese person to rule as emperor of China (1279–1294). Kublai Khan encouraged the advancement of literature, the arts and science and his court attracted people from countries all over the world. Page 4.

# L

**Lake Eufaula:** a lake in the eastern part of Oklahoma, a state in the south central part of the United States. Page 110.

**lamaseries, Tibetan:** monasteries of *lamas,* priests or monks in *Lamaism,* a branch of Buddhism that seeks to find release from the suffering of life and attain a state of complete happiness and peace. Lamaism originated in Tibet. Page 4.

**La Quinta:** a desert community located in Southern California. Page 79.

**larceny:** the unlawful taking and removing of another's personal property with the intent of permanently depriving the owner; theft. Page 87.

**Leeuwkop:** a prison located north of Johannesburg, a city in the northeastern part of South Africa. Page 122.

**Lesser Antilles:** islands of the West Indies that extend in an arc from Puerto Rico to the northeastern coast of South America. Page 78.

**lieutenant (jg):** *lieutenant junior grade,* a commissioned officer in the US Navy who is directly above an ensign, the lowest commissioned officer, and directly below a lieutenant. (A *commission* is a document conferring authority to officers in the army, navy and other military services, issued by the president of the United States.) Page 44.

**lodge:** become fixed, implanted or caught in a place or position; come to rest; stick. Page 105.

**LORAN:** abbreviation for LOng RAnge Navigation, a radio navigation system where the position of a ship or aircraft can be established based on the amount of time it takes radio signals to reach the ship from two or more known locations. Page 3.

**lore:** acquired knowledge or wisdom on a particular subject, for example, local traditions, handed down by word of mouth and usually in the form of stories or historical anecdotes. Page 20.

**Los Angeles earthquake:** a 6.7 magnitude earthquake that occurred approximately 20 miles (31 kilometers) from downtown Los Angeles, California, in 1994. It resulted in more than fifty deaths and many billions in property damage. Damage occurred up to 85 miles (125 kilometers) from the center of the earthquake. Page 118.

**Los Angeles riots:** civil violence in Los Angeles, California, in 1992, that resulted in more than fifty deaths and many millions in property damage. The riots occurred following a court decision that released four white police officers accused of beating a black motorist in 1991. Page 118.

**Lovecraft, H. P.:** Howard Phillips Lovecraft (1890–1937), American author of fantasy and horror stories. With fiction first published in the early 1920s, Lovecraft became known for his fascination with dark forces in settings that sometimes seem realistic and other times seem dreamlike. Page 34.

**LSD:** a drug that causes a person to have changes of thought processes, mood and perceptions. In addition to causing frightening experiences, LSD also causes *flashbacks,* visual disturbances that occur long after one has taken the drug. *LSD* is an abbreviation for the chemical compound *lysergic acid diethylamide.* Page 105.

**lucid(ly):** clear and easily understood. Page 102.

# M

**MacArthur, General Douglas:** (1880–1964) United States military commander, supreme commander of the armed forces in the Southwest Pacific during World War II (1939–1945). Page 44.

**magnate:** literally, a person having wealth and influence; also, a business, enterprise or the like having influence or distinction. Page 41.

**magnum opus:** a large or important literary work. A Latin expression, the term literally means great work. Page 80.

**Maharajah of Jaipur:** Sawai Man Singh II (1912–1970), the last ruler of Jaipur in India, before India became a republic in 1950, and owner of Saint Hill Manor during the 1950s. A *maharajah* is a former title used in India for a king or prince, especially the ruler of one of the larger regions. *Jaipur* is a former state in northwestern India, now part of the state of Rajasthan. It is also the name of the chief city of the region, now the capital of Rajasthan. Page 64.

**main, in the:** for the most part; mainly. Page 158.

**mainstay:** a thing that acts as a chief support or part. Page 109.

**Malaysia:** a country in Southeast Asia. It consists of two geographical regions divided by the South China Sea. Page 163.

***Management Series, The:*** a series of writings by L. Ron Hubbard that lay out his discoveries in the field of organization. Page 76.

**Mandarin:** the standard literary and official form of the Chinese language. Page 163.

**manuscript:** an author's work as written or typed, not a printed book. Page 5.

**maritime:** of or relating to sea navigation. Page 3.

**marketplace, closed:** a world or sphere of a particular business, trade or profession in which the persons involved are not willing to let newcomers have a role. Page 145.

**master mariner:** also *master* or *captain,* a person licensed to command a nonnaval ship. *Master mariners* are those individuals with demonstrated competence in such skills as emergency and safety operation, navigation, meteorology (the science of the atmosphere, weather and weather forecasting), radar, radio communication, ship handling, cargo operations and equipment, and maritime law. Page 42.

**Master of Sail Vessels license:** a certificate of competency to take charge or command of a nonnaval sail ship. In order to obtain such a certificate, competence is required in such skills as emergency and safety operation, navigation, ship handling and the laws of the sea. Page 44.

**Master of Steam and Motor Vessels license:** a certificate of competency to take charge or command of a *motor vessel,* one operated by engines, as opposed to one operated by sails. In order to obtain such a certificate, competence is required in such skills as emergency and safety operation, navigation, ship handling and the laws of the sea. Page 42.

**matriculates:** enrolls in a college or university after having met entrance requirements, such as passing an entrance examination. Page 29.

**maxim:** a statement of a general rule or truth. Page 9.

**McCaffrey, Anne:** (1926–2011) one of the most successful and popular science fiction and fantasy authors in the latter half of the twentieth century. Best known for her *Dragonriders of Pern* series, she became the first woman to win the Hugo and Nebula Awards. McCaffrey served as a judge of the Writers of the Future Contest beginning in 1985. Page 145.

**M.D.:** abbreviation of Latin *Medicinae Doctor,* Doctor of Medicine; a physician. Page 107.

**mechanistic:** explaining human behavior or other natural processes only in terms of physical causes or operating on such a principle without reference to spiritual aspects of existence. Page 88.

**medium:** a method that an artist uses or a category, such as film, in which an artist works. Page 140.

**Melbourne:** a city on the southern coast of Australia and the location of a Church of Scientology organization. Page 140.

**merit badges:** insignia granted by the Boy Scouts, worn especially on a uniform to indicate special achievement. Page 23.

**message:** the meaning, lesson or important idea that somebody wants to communicate—for example, in a work of art. Page 143.

**metabolite(s):** an altered form of a drug after it has been ingested and has undergone various chemical changes in the body. It is a waste product that is usually more or less toxic to the body. Page 107.

**metaphorically:** using a figure of speech in which a word or phrase is applied to something to which it is not literally applicable in order to suggest a resemblance. Page 8.

**meteoric:** developing very fast and attracting a lot of attention. Page 58.

**methadone:** a powerful synthetic drug developed in the 1940s. Methadone has been used as a substitute drug in the "treatment" of addiction to heroin, but persons using it end up addicted to it. The drug also causes other side effects, for example, affecting breathing and digestion. Page 109.

**methodology:** the methods or organizing principles underlying a particular art, science or other area of study. Page 4.

**µg/ml:** symbols meaning *microgram per milliliter*. A *microgram* is a unit of mass or weight equal to one millionth (*micro* = millionth, symbol µ) of a gram. (A gram weighs approximately .035 ounce.) A *milliliter* is a unit of volume equal to one thousandth of a liter. (A *liter* is equal to 34 ounces.) Page 107.

**Michigan:** a state in the north central United States. Page 31.

**Midwest:** the northern region of the central United States. Page 29.

**Mikvé Israel–Emanuel Synagogue:** the house of worship (synagogue) built in 1732 in Curaçao for the Mikvé Israel (Hope of Israel) congregation. This congregation, founded in 1651 by settlers from Amsterdam, Holland, is the oldest active Jewish congregation in the Americas. Page 78.

**milestone:** a significant or important event or stage in the life, progress, development or the like of a person, subject, Mankind, etc. A *milestone* is a stone or pillar set up to show the distance in miles to or from a specific place. Page 3.

**mixing:** electronically combining or blending various recorded or live instruments, voices and/or sounds to form a complete performance as one would hear in a concert or an album. Page 158.

**ml, µg/:** symbols meaning *microgram per milliliter*. A *microgram* is a unit of mass or weight equal to one millionth (*micro* = millionth, symbol µ) of a gram. (A gram weighs approximately .035 ounce.) A *milliliter* is a unit of volume equal to one thousandth of a liter. (A *liter* is equal to 34 ounces.) Page 107.

**molecular physics:** the branch of physics (science concerned with the nature and properties of matter and energy) that is involved with the study of atoms and molecules, their structure and energy and the relationships between them. An *atom* is a very small particle that is considered the building block of physical matter. *Molecules* are more complex structures formed by combinations of atoms. Page 29.

**monosyllabic:** composed primarily of short, simple words or of words that have only one syllable. Page 97.

**moral code:** an agreed-upon code of right and wrong conduct. Page 1.

**mother lode:** a plentiful supply of something having great value, from the literal idea of a *mother lode,* the main deposit of gold in a particular region or district. Page 161.

**multiple exposure:** a photograph made by the repeated exposure of the same frame of a film so as to produce superimposed images. Page 132.

**mushroomed:** sprang up suddenly or increased rapidly in numbers. Page 8.

**muster:** call up something; summon up something, such as strength or courage, that will help in doing something. Page 113.

**myriad:** a great number of things. Page 171.

***Mysterious Pilot, The:*** a 1937 movie serial, noted for its flying scenes, including plane crashes. The part of the hero was played by aviation pioneer Frank Hawks (1897–1938), holder of an early record for fastest flying time across the United States. Page 37.

# N

**namesake:** person having the same name as another. Page 19.

**Nantes:** a city in western France, important as a shipping and commercial center since ancient times. The city is also home to one of France's premier museums of fine art, the Musée des Beaux-Arts, which has one of the most important and varied collections of paintings in the country. Page 153.

**narcopolitical:** relating to or involving the combination or interaction of narcotics-related and political factors. Page 119.

**National Book Award:** any of the literary awards presented annually to authors in the United States in such areas as poetry, fiction and nonfiction. The National Book Awards are designed to advance the field of literature and enhance the cultural value of good writing in America. Page 146.

**National Boys' Week:** an event started in New York City in 1920 to help youth in the areas of education, citizenship, health and work. Page 23.

**National Endowment for the Arts:** an agency of the United States Government established in 1965 to award grants in support of artistic and innovative works that benefit individuals and communities. Page 146.

***National Geographic:*** an illustrated US magazine of geography, travel, science and exploration, published since 1888. Known internationally, it has one of the largest annual magazine circulations in the world. Along with colorful articles and exceptional photographs on people, places, animals, plants and natural wonders, the magazine also reports on significant explorations sponsored by its publisher, the *National Geographic Society,* a world-renowned organization founded in 1888 by a number of famous explorers and scientists for the increase and spreading of geographic knowledge. Page 3.

**National Guard:** in the United States, the military forces of the individual states, which can be called into active service for emergencies, for national defense, as a police force or the like. Page 24.

**national proliferation:** the rapid spread or increase of something throughout an entire country. Page 119.

**Naval School of Military Government:** a school of military government established at Princeton University, Princeton, New Jersey, in October 1944. The purpose was to train navy officers so as to provide needed personnel for projected military government activities as well as for specialized civilian duties. Page 44.

**naval yard:** also *navy yard,* a navy-owned *shipyard,* a place where warships are built and repaired. Page 23.

**navigation(al):** the science of locating the position of ships or aircraft and plotting and directing their course (the route along which a vessel or aircraft proceeds); directing a ship by determining its position, course and distance traveled. Navigation is concerned with finding the way, avoiding collision, meeting schedules, etc. Navigation uses various tools (such as charts; observation of the Sun, Moon and stars; and various electronic and mechanical instruments) and methods to determine a ship's direction and verify its position. Derived from the Latin *navis,* ship, and *agere,* to drive (literally, ship driving). Page 3.

**Nebula:** one of the major prizes for science fiction literature (Nebula Award) initiated in 1965. The Nebula is given by the Science Fiction and Fantasy Writers of America for the best writing in the fields of science fiction and fantasy published in the United States during the previous year. Page 146.

**nee:** a French term meaning born as, used to introduce a married woman's maiden name. Page 19.

**Netherlands Antilles:** islands in the Caribbean that are a part of the Kingdom of the Netherlands, having formerly been colonies. Page 153.

**newsreel:** a short motion picture film of news, current affairs and entertainment played in cinemas to moviegoers. Newsreels fell out of use in the late 1950s with the advent of television. Page 31.

**9/11:** September 11 (9/11), 2001, the date that the *World Trade Center,* a complex in New York City that included twin skyscrapers (the tallest in the US at 110 stories), was destroyed when two jetliners, hijacked by terrorists, were flown into the towers, causing the worst building disaster in recorded history and the deaths of some 2,800 people. Page 107.

**Niven, Larry:** Laurence van Cott Niven (1938– ), American science fiction author who began his professional speculative fiction writing career in 1964. He has authored and coauthored dozens of novels, including the Hugo and Nebula Award-winning *Ringworld* and (with Jerry Pournelle) the national bestsellers *The Mote in God's Eye, Lucifer's Hammer* and *Footfall.* Niven has been a Writers of the Future Contest judge since 1985. Page 145.

**novelette(s):** a brief novel. A *novel* is a work of fiction usually divided into chapters, often with a complex plot, in which the story develops through the action, speech and thoughts of its characters. Page 37.

**nuclear physics:** that branch of physics that deals with the behavior, structure and component parts of the center of an atom (called a *nucleus*). Page 4.

# O

**Oak Knoll Naval Hospital:** a naval hospital located in Oakland, California, where LRH spent time recovering from injuries sustained during World War II (1939–1945) and researching the effect of the mind on the physical recovery of patients. Page 5.

**Oakland:** a seaport in western California, on San Francisco Bay, opposite the city of San Francisco. Page 5.

**occupational forces:** the troops assigned to maintain control of a newly conquered region until the conclusion of hostilities or establishment of a settled government. Page 44.

**offing, in the:** expected or likely in the future. Page 61.

**oft:** an older word meaning often. Page 151.

**Ohio:** a state in the north central United States. Page 115.

**Oklahoma:** a state in the south central part of the United States. Page 110.

**omnipresent:** present in all places at the same time. Page 61.

**onerous:** burdensome, oppressive or troublesome; causing hardship. Page 125.

**opiates:** any drug made from or containing opium. *Opium* is an addictive drug prepared from the juice of a poppy. Some opiates are illegal and affect mood and behavior; others are used in medicine for relieving severe pain. Page 109.

**optic nerve(s):** the nerve that carries signals from the eye to the brain. *Optic* means of or relating to the eye or vision. Page 5.

**orchestrated:** worked out the parts of a piece of music to be performed by each instrument, as in a band or other performing group, done to prepare the music for an audience. Page 149.

**Organizing Board, Seven Division Scientology:** the chart, developed by L. Ron Hubbard, showing the pattern of organization and every function relative to successful group activity. The Organizing Board contains seven divisions, each with specific duties and functions. Page 73.

**Oriental:** in reference to styles of music found in the countries of the East, usually characterized by the sounds of particular instruments and drums, which sometimes give a quiet or sad tone, by a quality of sliding from one note to the next, as opposed to hitting each note directly and by little use of harmony in musical pieces. Page 149.

**outstrip:** exceed, surpass or be greater than. Page 78.

# P

**Pacific Northwest:** an area of the United States that includes the states of Washington, Oregon, Idaho and western Montana. Page 4.

**pantheon:** a group of people who are the most famous or respected in a particular field. Page 34.

**parameter:** a fact or circumstance that explains how something is done or what can be done. Page 107.

**Peking:** former name of Beijing, the capital of China. Page 25.

**Pentecostal Church:** a Christian church whose members strictly follow the Bible. Their beliefs and practices started from a religious revival in the United States in the early 1900s. Page 118.

**per se:** by or in itself, essentially; without reference to anything else. Page 61.

**P.H., Dr.:** an abbreviation for *Doctor of Public Health*. The field of *public health* includes areas such as health education, the prevention and control of diseases, environmental safety and pollution control. Page 107.

**Philippine:** of the *Philippines,* a country occupying a group of approximately 7,100 islands (Philippine Islands) in the southwestern Pacific Ocean off the southeast coast of Asia. Page 4.

**Philosophy of Language:** the branch of philosophy that analyzes basic concepts in language, such as meaning, communication and truth, and the connection between mind, language and the world. Page 99.

**phonetic:** having to do with *phonetics,* the study of speech sounds, their production and combination, and their representation by written symbols. Page 100.

**photojournalist:** a person involved in *photojournalism,* the communicating of news by photographs. Page 153.

**physical science:** any of the sciences, such as physics and chemistry, that study and analyze the nature and properties of energy and nonliving matter. Page 6.

**physiological(ly):** relating to the way living bodies function. Page 7.

**physiological response:** *physiological* means relating to the way living bodies function. *Response* means something done as a reaction to some influence, event, etc. *Physiological response* means outward physical signs or indications as a reaction (to something). Page 93.

**Pietermaritzburg:** a city in eastern South Africa. Page 118.

**pirated:** used or reproduced (another's work) for profit without permission. Page 87.

**pivotal:** of vital or critical importance. Page 41.

**plunked down:** set down abruptly. Page 97.

**Pohl, Frederik:** (1919– ) American science fiction writer and editor whose decades-long career has resulted in many achievements in the science fiction field. Not only has his editorship of science fiction magazines been recognized with several Hugo Awards, but his writings also have won both Hugo and Nebula Awards. Page 137.

**pollutants, airborne:** chemicals or waste products that contaminate the environment and that are *airborne,* carried along by movements of air. Page 107.

**Port Orchard:** a resort and fishing community located in western Washington State on *Puget Sound,* a long, narrow bay of the Pacific Ocean on the northwestern coast of the United States. Page 34.

**port(s) of call:** a harbor town or city where ships can visit during the course of a voyage. Page 78.

**postulated:** assumed to be true, real or necessary, especially as a basis for reasoning. Page 29.

**postulating:** considering or saying a thing and having it be true. Page 135.

**Pournelle, Jerry:** (1933– ) American author, essayist and journalist. He has written numerous science fiction novels, including the national bestselling *The Mote in God's Eye, Lucifer's Hammer* and *Footfall.* Pournelle has edited many anthologies and written a range of nonfiction pieces for the speculative fiction media. A past president of the Science Fiction Writers of America, he has been a Writers of the Future judge since 1986. Page 145.

**pragmatic:** concerned with actual practice, not with theory or speculation; practical. Page 114.

**precedence:** the condition of having greater importance than something else; priority in importance, order or rank. Page 6.

**precepts:** rules, instructions or principles that guide somebody's actions, especially ones that guide moral behavior. Page 114.

**precipitating:** bringing about the occurrence of something, especially suddenly or rapidly. Page 76.

**precipitously:** falling with extreme rapidity. Page 83.

**preclear:** from *pre-Clear,* a person not yet Clear; generally a person being audited, who is thus on the road to *Clear,* the name of a state achieved through auditing or an individual who has achieved this state. The Clear is an unaberrated person who has cleared the destructive impulses of the reactive mind. Page 50.

**preconceiving:** imagining beforehand; anticipating in thought. Page 154.

**prefaced:** included an introductory statement in a book, such as one that lays out the purpose or scope of the book. Page 118.

**prescribing:** laying down as a course of action to be followed. Page 106.

**Princeton University:** a leading United States university, located in Princeton, New Jersey. In the 1940s, it housed a Naval School of Military Government to train navy officers and provide needed personnel for projected military government activities. Page 44.

**probation department:** a section of a criminal justice system that deals with the supervision of criminal offenders after their release from prison or as an alternative to prison. *Probation* means the supervision of the behavior of a young or first-time criminal offender by an authorized person (probation officer). During the period of supervision, the offender must regularly report to the probation officer and must not commit any further offenses. Page 47.

**processing:** the application of Dianetics or Scientology techniques (called *processes*). Page 7.

**proclamation:** something that is announced or declared; a public, official announcement. Page 165.

**prodigious:** extraordinary in size, amount, extent or degree. Page 140.

**profound(ly):** deep-reaching or very great. Page 3.

**proliferation, national:** the rapid spread or increase of something throughout an entire country. Page 119.

**prolific:** producing large quantities of something or with great frequency. Page 2.

**protectorship:** used with reference to the status of Puerto Rico, an island in the Caribbean under the protection of the United States but having independence and self-government in local matters and only partial control over foreign affairs. Page 2.

**prototypic:** of or being a *prototype,* the original or model on which other things are based or formed. Page 42.

**pseudonym(s):** a fictitious name assumed by an author; pen name. Page 141.

**psychedelic:** of or relating to the time period or culture associated with *psychedelic drugs,* those drugs (such as LSD) capable of producing hallucinations and other abnormal psychic effects resembling mental illness. Page 105.

**psychic:** having to do with the psyche. *Psyche* is the Greek word meaning breath of life, mind or soul. Page 157.

**psychosomatic:** *psycho* refers to mind and *somatic* refers to body; the term *psychosomatic* means the mind making the body ill or illnesses which have been created physically within the body by the mind. A description of the cause and source of psychosomatic ills is contained in *Dianetics: The Modern Science of Mental Health*. Page 7.

**public domain:** the condition of being openly known or publicized. Page 146.

***Publishers Weekly:*** an international newsmagazine for the book publishing and bookselling industry. It provides news on the publishing industry, with data on bestsellers, statistics and annual reviews of several thousand books. It is subscribed to by bookstores, libraries, media and publishers. Page 161.

**Puerto Rican mineralogical survey:** also known as the *West Indies Mineralogical Expedition*, an expedition organized and conducted by L. Ron Hubbard during the early 1930s. The expedition also toured other Caribbean islands while conducting its primary mission, the first complete mineralogical survey of Puerto Rico under United States protectorship. Page 2.

**Puget Sound:** a long, narrow bay of the Pacific Ocean on the coast of Washington, a state in the northwestern United States. Page 23.

**pulmonary:** of or pertaining to the lungs. Page 107.

**pulp fiction:** the adventure, science fiction, cowboy stories and the like published during the early 1900s. Produced in magazines printed on inexpensive, rough-surfaced paper, pulp fiction had a wide audience. Page 34.

**pulpwood stock:** the rough type of paper (stock) used for printing inexpensive magazines, etc. The low-cost pulp used in its manufacture is made from wood fibers, which give a rough texture. Page 137.

**Purification Program:** a program to purify and clean out of one's system the restimulative drug or chemical residues that could act to prevent gains from Dianetics and Scientology processing. *See also* **processing.** Page 79.

**putrefaction:** the state of having deteriorated or decayed. Page 10.

# Q

**quarter:** a particular but unspecified person, group, area or place. Page 3.

**quelling:** suppressing; putting an end to. Page 119.

# R

**radioactive fallout:** airborne radioactive dust and material shot into the atmosphere by a nuclear explosion which then settles to the ground. *Radioactive* describes a substance that sends out harmful energy in the form of streams of very small particles due to the decay (breaking down) of atoms within the substance. Page 61.

**radio directional finding:** the act or practice of determining the direction from which radio waves or signals are coming, often using a device such as an antenna that can be rotated freely on a vertical axis. Radio directional finding is usually used to assist in determining a ship's position. Page 3.

**radio navigation system:** a reference to *radio directional finding. See also* **radio directional finding.** Page 42.

**ramifications:** effects, consequences or results that follow an action or decision. Page 6.

**reactive mind:** that portion of a person's mind which is entirely stimulus-response, which is not under his volitional control and which exerts force and the power of command over his awareness, purposes, thoughts, body and actions. Page 7.

**realized:** presented or brought before the mind with vividness and clarity. Page 8.

**recalcitrant:** resisting authority or control; not obedient or compliant. Page 102.

**recidivism:** repeated or habitual relapse into criminal habits. Page 83.

**referendum:** the submission of a law, proposed or already in effect, to a direct vote of the people. Page 119.

**reggae:** a style of rhythmic Jamaican popular music blending blues, calypso and rock-and-roll. Page 149.

**regimen:** a prescribed or regulated program. Page 76.

**reigned:** had widespread influence and impact. Page 139.

**renaissance:** any revival or period of marked improvement and new life, in philosophy, art, literature, etc. Page 101.

**replete:** abundantly supplied or provided; filled. Page 3.

**replicate:** do (something) again or copy (something); reproduce. Page 163.

**resonance:** an intensified effect, such as of an event or work of art, beyond what is immediately apparent; underlying significance. Page 113.

**restive:** uneasy, resisting or difficult to control. Page 119.

**retrospective:** marked by a looking back over past situations, events, etc. Page 161.

**Rhodesia:** a country in Africa, now called Zimbabwe. Page 75.

**Rich, Buddy:** (1917–1987) American jazz drummer and bandleader billed as "the world's greatest drummer." Known for his brilliant technique, power and speed, he played with several big bands, started several short-lived bands of his own and often performed solo. Page 149.

**rife with:** full of or severely affected by something undesirable. Page 158.

**riots, Los Angeles:** civil violence in Los Angeles, California, in 1992, that resulted in more than fifty deaths and many millions in property damage. The riots occurred following a court decision that released four white police officers accused of beating a black motorist in 1991. Page 118.

**rollicking:** exuberantly lively and amusing. Page 142.

**romance:** 1. a story in which the emphasis is on love. Page 34.
2. the type of stories that describe exciting and heroic deeds and adventures, usually in a historical or imaginary setting. Page 137.

**Rwanda:** a small country in east central Africa, just south of the equator. Page 122.

# S

**saga:** a long story or series of incidents, often one of adventures, heroic events or the like. Page 80.

**Saint Hill Manor:** a manor (a large house and its land) located in East Grinstead, Sussex, in southern England. Saint Hill Manor was the residence of L. Ron Hubbard as well as the international communications and training center of Scientology from the late 1950s through the mid-1960s. Page 64.

**Saint Hill Special Briefing Course:** a course conducted by L. Ron Hubbard at Saint Hill in England. From 1961 until 1966, he regularly lectured to the students on this course and personally oversaw their training. All of Mr. Hubbard's lectures were recorded and today the Saint Hill Special Briefing Course is delivered by a number of Scientology organizations around the world with students studying the same writings and lectures provided by Mr. Hubbard originally. Page 69.

**Salon International d'Art Photographique:** an international photography exhibit held in Versailles, a city in northern France, about 12 miles (19 kilometers) southwest of Paris. Page 153.

**sanctioned:** authorized, approved or allowed. Page 119.

**sans:** a French word meaning without or lacking. Page 101.

**satire:** a literary work that uses humor and ridicule to expose stupidity, abuses, etc. Page 150.

**Scholastic Aptitude Test:** also known as the *Scholastic Assessment Tests,* examination required by most higher-education institutions in the United States for admission into college. The test is designed to assess math, verbal and reasoning abilities. Page 91.

**schooner:** a sailing ship with sails set lengthwise (fore and aft) and having from two to as many as seven masts. Page 27.

**science, physical:** any of the sciences, such as physics and chemistry, that study and analyze the nature and properties of energy and nonliving matter. Page 6.

**Scientology:** the term Scientology is taken from the Latin *scio,* which means "knowing in the fullest sense of the word," and the Greek word *logos,* meaning "study of." In itself the word means literally "knowing how to know." Scientology is further defined as the study and handling of the spirit in relationship to itself, universes and other life. Page 1.

***Scientology: The Fundamentals of Thought:*** a book written by L. Ron Hubbard in 1956. *Scientology: The Fundamentals of Thought* is the Basic Book on the theory and practice of Scientology. Page 61.

**score:** adapt (a piece of music) for a particular style of performance by voices or instruments; arrange. Page 81.

**scourge:** something that causes widespread or great trouble or misery. Page 97.

**screenwriter:** the writer of a script that is intended to be filmed. Page 140.

**script:** write or prepare a *script,* the text of a film, play or radio or television broadcast, including the words to be spoken and often also technical directions. Page 79.

**scriptures:** the sacred writings of a religion. Page 8.

**Sea Organization:** the religious order of the Scientology religion, consisting of Scientologists who have pledged themselves to eternal service. The Sea Organization derives its name from its beginnings in 1967 when Sea Org members lived and worked aboard a flotilla of ships. Page 75.

**secular:** of or pertaining to things that are not regarded as religious or sacred. Page 71.

**security (maximum, medium, minimum):** *security* refers to the ranking of a prison, based on the degree of protection or defense against escape. *Maximum security prisons* generally hold prisoners serving long sentences for serious crimes such as murder, robbery, kidnapping or the like. *Medium security prisons* hold prisoners convicted of less serious crimes, such as assaults and small thefts. *Minimum security prisons* are for people convicted of nonviolent crimes, such as cheating on taxes. Page 121.

**seeded:** filled or furnished with something that grows or stimulates growth or development. Page 119.

**seminal:** highly influential in the development of future events. Page 109.

**serial:** any of the short movies shown as a series of up to fifteen separate installments, often in conjunction with a full-length film. These short films, each with a dramatic ending, drew the audience back each week for the next exciting chapter in the story. Page 37.

**service industry:** the types of businesses that provide personal and professional services to others but that are not involved in manufacturing. Examples of such businesses are banks, hotels and restaurants. Page 130.

**set design:** the combination of artistic details or architectural features that make up a *set,* a construction representing a place, room or scene in which the action takes place in a stage, motion picture or television production. Page 157.

**Seven Division Scientology Organizing Board:** the chart, developed by L. Ron Hubbard, showing the pattern of organization and every function relative to successful group activity. The Organizing Board contains seven divisions, each with specific duties and functions. Page 73.

**seven seas:** a reference to all the seas and oceans of the world or a great expanse of water in general. Throughout the centuries, the term has been used for the various seas and oceans known to people at the time. Page 42.

**shaman:** a priest or priestess who is said to act as an intermediary between natural and supernatural worlds and to use magic to cure ailments, foretell the future and to contact and control spiritual forces. Page 20.

**sheer:** the most complete and utter (used to emphasize the unlimited extent of something). Page 11.

**short, in:** introducing a summary statement of what has been previously stated in a few words; in summary. Page 7.

**shrill:** marked by a sharp insistence on being heard; demanding. Page 119.

**Shrine Auditorium:** a landmark auditorium in Los Angeles, California. Built in the 1920s, the Shrine is one of the largest enclosed theaters in the United States, with a stage almost 200 feet (65 meters) wide and with seating for more than 6,000 people. Page 48.

**sibling(s):** a brother or sister. Page 19.

**signpost:** literally, a long piece of wood or other material set upright into the ground bearing a sign that gives information or directions, such as the proper road to a place or the like. Hence, any immediate indication, obvious clue, guide, etc. Page 5.

**Silverberg, Robert:** (1935– ) American author of hundreds of science fiction stories and more than a hundred novels. Widely published since the 1950s, he has won five Nebula Awards and five Hugo Awards and was named a Grand Master by the Science Fiction Writers of America in 2004. In addition to his extensive writing career, he has been a Writers of the Future Contest judge since its first year in 1984. Page 145.

**single:** a short record with one song on each side. Page 150.

**socioeconomic:** of or involving both social and economic factors such as work experience and economic or social position, based on income, education and occupation. Page 93.

**sojourn:** a temporary stay. Page 24.

**sonic:** relating to or using sound; hence audible to the human ear. Page 161.

**Soweto:** a township in northeastern South Africa, located 15 miles (24 kilometers) southwest of Johannesburg, the largest city in the country. The name Soweto stands for South-Western Townships. Page 118.

**Spanish Lake:** the international headquarters and training campus of Applied Scholastics International, located in Spanish Lake, a community near St. Louis, Missouri, in the central United States. Page 103.

**Special Officer:** a patrol officer licensed by the police department. Special Officers either remain in a specific area to guard it or patrol a neighborhood on behalf of the local merchants. They are armed, uniformed and generally have the same duties as a regular police officer when on patrol. Page 47.

**speculative:** of writing that is usually considered to include fantasy, horror, science fiction and the like, dealing with worlds unlike the real world. Page 141.

**spell out:** explain something simply and in detail. Page 129.

***Spider Returns, The:*** a 1941 movie serial based on the crime-fighting character the Spider, from the pulp magazine stories of author Norvell Page (1904–1961). *The Spider Returns* was a sequel to an earlier serial, *The Spider's Web,* based on the adventures of the same character. Page 37.

***Sportsman Pilot, The:*** a monthly American aviation magazine published from around 1930 until 1943. It contained writings on a wide range of subjects, including coverage of aerial sporting events, commentary on current aviation issues, technical articles on flying as well as other articles on topics of general interest. Page 29.

**Standard Magazines:** a publishing company that produced a number of well-known pulp magazines, such as *Thrilling Adventures, Thrilling Detective, Thrilling Western, Startling Stories* and others. Operating from the 1930s to the early 1960s, the company was also called Thrilling Publications, Beacon Magazines and Better Publications. Page 140.

**Stanislavsky:** stage name of Konstantin Sergeyevich Alekseyev (1863–1938), Russian actor, producer, director and teacher. Page 157.

**status quo:** the state in which something is: the existing state of affairs, usually implying one that is unchanging as desired by certain groups or individuals. Page 135.

**stewardship:** conduct of the office of *steward,* someone who manages the property or finances of another; management; control. Page 161.

**stimulus-response:** a certain stimulus (something that rouses a person or thing to activity or energy or that produces a reaction in the body) automatically giving a certain response. Page 7.

**stint:** a period of time spent doing something. Page 140.

**storm, taking by:** creating a great impression upon; captivating; becoming quickly popular or famous. Page 7.

**Street & Smith:** a large American publishing company established in the mid-1800s that put out a large number of periodicals and pulp magazines in the late nineteenth and early twentieth centuries, such as *Astounding Science Fiction* magazine and *Unknown* magazine. Page 41.

**strokes, broad:** literally, a wide mark of a pen or pencil when writing or a brush when painting. Hence *broad strokes,* a general view or picture of a topic or subject. Page 3.

**Study Technology:** the term given to the methods developed by L. Ron Hubbard that enable individuals to study effectively. It is an exact technology that anyone can use to learn a subject or to acquire a new skill. It provides an understanding of the fundamental principles of how to learn and gives precise ways to overcome the barriers and pitfalls one can encounter during study, such as going by misunderstood words or symbols. Page 71.

**stumbling block:** an obstacle or hindrance to progress or understanding. Page 99.

**subchaser:** a shortening of *submarine chaser,* a small patrol vessel, usually 100–200 feet (30–60 meters) long, designed for military operations against submarines. Page 44.

**subjectively:** in a way that is experienced personally, as an individual. Page 9.

**suite(s):** a group of rooms designed to be used together. Page 93.

**suit, follow:** do the same as something else has done; follow an example set. Page 48.

**sum and substance:** main idea or essence (of something). Page 122.

**supercargo:** an officer who is in charge of the cargo and commercial matters aboard a merchant ship. Page 27.

**supermax:** describing a prison that is made secure by the most extensive and elaborate security arrangements that are available or in current use. Page 122.

**Sussex:** a county of southeastern England. Saint Hill is located in East Grinstead, Sussex. Page 64.

**switchboard:** literally, a board containing switches and other devices for controlling electric flows, used to connect and disconnect communication lines. Used figuratively in reference to the brain, which functions as the control center of the nervous system by receiving information from the senses, analyzing it and deciding how the body should respond. Page 106.

**symphonic:** of or having to do with harmony of sound, such as from a *symphony orchestra,* a large orchestra that includes many different instruments playing together. Page 151.

**synergy:** combined or cooperative action or force. Page 163.

**synthesizer:** any of various electronic consoles or modules, usually computerized, used to produce sounds unobtainable from ordinary musical instruments or to imitate instruments and voices. Page 150.

# T

**Tagalogs:** members of the ethnic group that is native to Manila (seaport and capital of the Philippines) and the surrounding region. Page 4.

**"tapestry":** figuratively, something that is rich, varied or intricately interwoven, likened to a *tapestry,* a piece of strong cloth decorated with pictures that are painted, embroidered or woven in colors, used for a wall hanging. Page 150.

**technology:** the methods of application of an art or science as opposed to mere knowledge of the science or art itself. In Scientology, the term *technology* refers to the methods of application of Scientology principles to improve the functions of the mind and rehabilitate the potentials of the spirit, developed by L. Ron Hubbard. Page 2.

**tenet(s):** something accepted as an important truth; any of a set of established and fundamental beliefs, such as one relating to religion. Page 8.

**Tennant, Forest:** noted physician and author who started a pain clinic in 1975. A former army medical officer, Dr. Tennant has been a consultant to a number of government bodies, including the US Food and Drug Administration, as well as to professional sports leagues. Page 107.

***Terra Incognita:*** an unknown or unexplored land, region or subject. The term is Latin for "unknown land." Page 47.

**thence:** from there; from that place. Page 24.

**thesis:** a systematic treatment of a subject that includes results of original research and establishes, by proof or evidence, the existence or truth of specific phenomena. Page 6.

**Thompson, Commander:** Joseph Cheesman Thompson (1874–1943), a commander and surgeon in the United States Navy who studied Freudian analysis with Sigmund Freud (1856–1939). Page 4.

***Thrilling Adventures:*** a pulp magazine produced by the publishing company of Thrilling Publications (also known as Standard Magazines, Beacon Magazines and Better Publications). The company also produced pulp magazines such as *Thrilling Detective, Thrilling Western, Startling Stories* and others. Page 141.

**Tibetan lamaseries:** monasteries of *lamas,* priests or monks in *Lamaism,* a branch of Buddhism that seeks to find release from the suffering of life and attain a state of complete happiness and peace. Lamaism originated in Tibet. Page 4.

**Tilden, Nebraska:** a town in the northeastern part of Nebraska, a state in the central part of the United States. Page 19.

**timbre:** the quality of a sound that distinguishes it from other sounds of the same pitch (high or low sounding) and volume (loud or soft). For example, the difference in timbre between a flute and a violin makes them sound different even if they play a note of the same pitch and with the same volume. Page 149.

**Tlingit:** a Native North American people of the coastal regions of southern Alaska and northern British Columbia, Canada. Page 42.

**tone:** the momentary or continuing emotional state of a person. Page 157.

**township:** (in South Africa) a segregated residential settlement for blacks, located outside a city or town. Page 118.

**trade school(s):** a school that gives instruction in skilled trades, such as carpentry or automobile repair. Page 93.

**traffic:** deal or trade (in something illegal). Page 109.

**transferring:** putting a track or several tracks together onto one final track. This is different than straight copying because it can involve mixing to get proper volume. Page 158.

**travail:** pain or suffering resulting from conditions that are mentally or physically difficult to overcome. Page 9.

**tribal medicine man:** a person believed to have supernatural powers of curing disease and controlling spirits, as in a *tribal group,* a local division of a Native North American people. Page 3.

# U

**United States Navy Reserve:** part of the United States Navy in which members, called *Reservists,* are registered with the navy and may be called into active duty as needed or required but who do not otherwise hold positions in the navy as a career. Page 44.

**unmitigated:** not lessened in force or intensity. Page 5.

**USS *Henderson:*** a United States naval transport vessel from 1917, when she transported troops to Europe during World War I (1914–1918), until her reassignment as a hospital ship in 1943 during World War II (1939–1945). During the 1920s and 1930s, the *Henderson* was primarily assigned transport duties in the Pacific Ocean. *USS* is an abbreviation for *United States Ship.* Page 27.

**USS *President Madison:*** a ship built in 1921, named after American president James Madison (1751–1836), on which LRH and his mother crossed the Pacific in 1927, visiting Hawaii, Japan, China and the Philippines. The final leg of their journey took them to the naval station in Guam. *USS,* as used on commercial vessels, is an abbreviation for *United States Steamship.* Page 24.

**USS *Ulysses S. Grant:*** a military transport ship that began service in 1917, during World War I (1914–1918). Her transport duties continued during the 1920s and 1930s, chiefly in the Pacific Ocean and through the Panama Canal. Her final service was during World War II (1939–1945). The ship was named for Ulysses S. Grant (1822–1885), Civil War general and eighteenth president of the United States (1869–1877). *USS* is an abbreviation for *United States Ship.* Page 23.

# V

**van Vogt, A. E.:** Alfred Elton van Vogt (1912–2000), Canadian-born science fiction writer who began his decades-long career during science fiction's Golden Age (1939–1949). Esteemed in the science fiction field, van Vogt was presented the Grand Master Award by the Science Fiction Writers of America in 1995. Page 142.

**vehemence:** the quality of being *vehement,* expressing something with conviction or intense feeling. Page 4.

**vehicle:** a medium of communication, expression or display. Page 137.

**vein:** a particular quality or characteristic. Page 29.

**veritable:** being truly or very much so. Page 34.

**Versailles:** a city in northern France, about 12 miles (19 kilometers) southwest of Paris. Versailles is particularly noted as the site of the palace and gardens of the kings of France, built in the 1600s, now a national museum. Page 153.

**Vienna:** the capital of Austria, where Sigmund Freud (1856–1939) founded psychoanalysis. Page 4.

**volitional:** of or related to the act of consciously choosing. Page 7.

# W

**wake of, in the:** *wake* is the visible trail (of agitated and disturbed water) left by something, such as a ship, moving through water. Hence a condition left behind someone or something that has passed; following as a consequence. Page 23.

***Washington Herald:*** an American newspaper published in Washington, DC, from 1906 to 1939. Page 29.

**washout curve:** the graphic representation of the change occurring over a period of time (curve) concerning the elimination of drugs or chemicals from the body (washout). Page 107.

**Watts:** a neighborhood in South Central Los Angeles, California, where high unemployment, poverty and social injustices led to riots in 1965. The area experienced a high incidence of drug-related gang violence from the 1970s through the early 1990s. Page 118.

**Western Hills:** a range of hills in China, situated northwest of the Chinese capital, Beijing. The range is known for its many temples and has long been a religious retreat. Page 4.

**whilst:** a chiefly British term meaning during the time that; while. Page 41.

**Williamson, Jack:** John Stewart Williamson (1908–2006), American science fiction writer named a Grand Master by the Science Fiction Writers of America. Author of numerous short stories and novels, his writing career spanned more than seven decades. Well known for his teaching and lecturing, Williamson was also an instructor at the original Writers of the Future workshop and for two decades he served as a judge of the Writers of the Future Contest. Page 145.

**Winchell, Walter:** (1897–1972) famous US journalist and broadcaster whose newspaper columns and radio news broadcasts gave him a massive audience and great influence in the United States in the 1930s, 1940s and 1950s. Page 6.

**wiping out:** removing or eliminating something, as when one sound cancels another sound. Page 149.

**wit, to:** used to introduce a list or explanation of what one has just mentioned. Originally a phrase used in law, *that is to wit,* which meant that is to know, that is to say. Page 87.

**WOL:** the group of letters (termed *call letters*) that identify a radio transmitting station, in this case a radio station located in Washington, DC. Radio WOL began operating in the late 1920s, making it one of the oldest radio stations in Washington, DC. Page 29.

**word, in a:** expressed in a concise way; briefly. Page 71.

**wrought:** brought about or caused. Page 105.

# Y

**yardstick:** a standard used to judge the quality, value or success of something. Page 5.

# INDEX

Old Tom, medicine man, 3, 20

*Black Mask,* 137

**blood brother**

L. Ron Hubbard and Blackfeet
Indians, 3, 20

**Boy Scouts**

Eagle Scout, nation's youngest, 23

Washington, DC, 23

Washington State, 23

**Bridge, Scientology,** 9, 71, 76

**British Columbia**

maritime guides, 3

**British government study report,** 91

*Buckskin Brigades,* 140, 161

Blackfeet Indians, 140

*New York Times* review of, 140

**Burks, Arthur J.,** 137

**Burroughs, Edgar Rice,** 34, 137

**businesses failing**

solutions, 125–131

# C

**calypso,** 149

**Camera Room**

L. Ron Hubbard, 154–155

**Card, Orson Scott**

Writers of the Future judge, 145

**Caribbean Motion Picture Expedition**

*Doris Hamlin,* 31

photographs sold to *New York Times,* 31

**cellular memory experiments,** 39

**Chandler, Raymond,** 34, 137

**Charlie Award,** 147

**Chicago, Illinois**

Hubbard Dianetic Research
Foundation, 48

**children**

Study Technology and, 93

today's children will become tomorrow's
civilization, 91

**China**

photograph of L. Ron Hubbard in
Peking, 25

royal magicians descended from the
court of Kublai Khan, 4

series of photographs on, 155

traveling to, 24, 27

Western Hills

Tibetan lamasery and, 4

**chronology**

L. Ron Hubbard, 17–83

**church choirs of every denomination**

rejuvenation of regional religious
influence and, 78

**civilization**

L. Ron Hubbard's search for solutions to
the cultural crises, 10

**Clarke, Stanley**

*Space Jazz* album, 150

**Classification and Gradation Chart,** 73

**Clear**

history of technical development
and, 69

state of, 7

*Clear Body, Clear Mind*

Purification Program and, 106

**Clearsound**

sound technology, 158

# THE
# L. RON HUBBARD
## SERIES

"To really know life," L. Ron Hubbard wrote, "you've got to be part of life. You must get down and look, you must get into the nooks and crannies of existence. You have to rub elbows with all kinds and types of men before you can finally establish what he is."

Through his long and extraordinary journey to the founding of Dianetics and Scientology, Ron did just that. From his adventurous youth in a rough and tumble American West to his far-flung trek across a still mysterious Asia; from his two-decade search for the very essence of life to the triumph of Dianetics and Scientology—such are the stories recounted in the L. Ron Hubbard Biographical Publications.

Drawn from his own archival collection, this is Ron's life as he himself saw it. With each volume of the series focusing upon a separate field of endeavor, here are the compelling facts, figures, anecdotes and photographs from a life like no other.

Indeed, here is the life of a man who lived at least twenty lives in the space of one.

FOR FURTHER INFORMATION VISIT
**www.lronhubbard.org**

To order copies of *The L. Ron Hubbard Series*
or L. Ron Hubbard's Dianetics and
Scientology books and lectures, contact:

US AND INTERNATIONAL

BRIDGE PUBLICATIONS, INC.
*5600 E. Olympic Blvd.*
*Commerce, California 90022 USA*
*www.bridgepub.com*
*Tel: (323) 888-6200*
*Toll-free: 1-800-722-1733*

UNITED KINGDOM AND EUROPE

NEW ERA PUBLICATIONS
INTERNATIONAL ApS
*Smedeland 20*
*2600 Glostrup, Denmark*
*www.newerapublications.com*
*Tel: (45) 33 73 66 66*
*Toll-free: 00-800-808-8-8008*